Personal Business

"We know that there are countless books, manuals, guides, and even talks that address balancing each aspect of one's life, be it personal, professional, spiritual, etc. I find that many of them are geared toward those who believe that the personal and the professional are fundamentally at odds with one another. In fact, most have been conditioned to accept that we must resign ourselves to the idea that one will necessarily prevent the other from thriving or that one cannot flourish except at the fatal expense of the other.

"The ASA Way is distinct in that, instead, it strives to foster an environment in which all areas of your life can prosper in a symbiotic relationship. Personally, I have found that the key to that is in the way we work and grow as one team in the workplace. I recall working as an associate attorney not long ago in another small firm where I was told that competition with your teammates is the way to get ahead, is a good thing, and can be exciting. Conveniently omitted from this bad advice is that it harbors toxic energy that ultimately manifests in nothing more than resentment.

"The ASA Way, however, does actually endorse competition—competition with oneself. To be better than you were yesterday as opposed to, for example, just bitter at your colleague. We seek to serve as inspirations rather than obstructions to each other. This source of support translates to positive alignment in all aspects of our lives. And all this means that we can better care for our clients, for each other, and for ourselves."

Attorney, ASA Law Group, California

"I had worked at other law firms prior to joining ASA Law Group; my workplace experiences at these other firms were the reason I ran toward ASA, hoping that the work culture really would be different there. The reason I was fleeing these prior firms was because toxic workplace dynamics had become the norm, causing division between employees. I left my first firm hoping for better; I thought maybe it was just that first firm's environment that was detrimental to productivity and my personal well-being, but sadly I was wrong. Staff and attorneys at the next firm were at opposition, and even within that dichotomy there was an inner circle that could not be penetrated without seniority. It became increasingly clear to me how this system played out for the peons when I was bullied by a peer, a grown woman, but the incident was brushed aside by my supervisor and deemed merely a joke. This was normal? This was going to be my day-to-day? I had to leave, as I could not accept the fact that every firm was run like this.

"I have never once felt unheard or unsupported since beginning work for ASA Law Group. The ASA Way values the individual team member. Each employee has a vital role, and there is not an us-versus-them mentality. We are one team. Communication and collaboration are encouraged and celebrated. You have a support system in place with managers, team leads, and an owner who understands we are human; some days we need more from each other than others, and that's okay. Knowing you have this support system changes not only your workdays but also your mindset. You no longer have the "Sunday scaries." Each obstacle put before you is solvable because you are given the tools to succeed, while also feeling valued in your role. The ASA Way makes you want to perform better and work harder for your company as an employee. I want my company to succeed, not only for my own personal and professional growth and the development of our firm, but also so I never have to go back to work for another toxic workplace again. I now have friends telling me they want what I have; they want happiness and support at their job. Employees are ready and in need of a change from the old workplace dynamics that stifle progress and success in an office setting. I hope more companies will be willing to give the ASA Way approach a chance. Your staff will thank you, perform for you, and be happy to go that extra mile when it's needed."

Beth Kelly, Director of Operations, ASA Law Group

"A wise woman (my mother) once told me to surround myself with people who talk about ideas and visions, not other people. In my youth, that never really landed. In adulthood, it's proven to be a benchmark in my life. When I am in either professional or personal environments, I always fall back on this. As an employee, I could never really find a place where I felt as though my work environment bettered me or enriched my life. It simply boiled down to being better than the competition. An adult game of "Keeping Up with the Joneses." My career quickly morphed into a joyless meal ticket to pay my bills and make ends meet.

"Then I ran into an old coworker who had branched off and started his own firm. Luckily for me, he was hiring. From the first interview, I could tell ASA Law Group would be different. It prioritized the individual worker. More so, it valued the personal values of each individual worker. From my first day on the job, I can honestly say that my firm cares more about me, my family, and my mental well-being than about me as the worker or employee. Year after year, I experience constant check-ins. Real check-ins—not the ones that follow an

HR script. My schedule is always accommodated when possible, and I am trusted to do my job without interference. If I need something, I have a safe and transparent environment to ask for it. My colleagues have become not just friends, but family.

"I never thought I would be able to find a work environment that enriched me as a person. However, ASA has not only made me a better worker but an overall better human. I am happy to come to work and (hopefully) pay the same in kind to my peers. We are a progressive, out-of-the-box firm that will never stop evolving and progressing to be better. I am proud just to be a working part of such an organization."

Attorney, ASA Law Group, Illinois

"My career as an attorney changed completely when I came to ASA. I had previously worked at more traditional firms, focused almost solely on performance and metrics. I always assumed that the burnout was a rite of passage in the legal field, but I still hoped to practice in an environment where I could grow as a person, not just as a lawyer. When the opportunity came to work at ASA, it was time to find out if there was a better way.

"Coming to ASA and experiencing the ASA Way as a leadership style proved that there was a different and better method to both legal practice and business management. Of course, efficiency and output are still put in high regard; a business cannot thrive without results and productivity. But the ASA Way focuses more deeply on the individual, fostering personal growth and well-being while simultaneously harvesting professional success. Since working at ASA, I truly feel this philosophy has inspired me not only to become a better lawyer and to want to master my craft but also to become a more well-rounded and holistic person. The ASA Way has the ability to change the legal field as we know it and beyond."

Attorney, ASA Law Group, Illinois

SHUAIB AHMED

Personal Business

Using the ASA Way to Build an
Inspired, Purposeful Team

SHUAIB AHMED

Personal Business

Using the ASA Way to Build an
Inspired, Purposeful Team

ForbesBooks

Published by ForbesBooks, Charleston, South Carolina.
Member of Advantage Media Group.

ForbesBooks is a registered trademark, and the ForbesBooks colophon is a trademark of Forbes Media, LLC.

Printed in the United States of America.

10 9 8 7 6 5 4 3 2 1

ISBN: 978-1-95588-412-9
LCCN: 2021925557

Cover design by David Taylor.
Layout design by Wesley Strickland.

Advantage Media Group is proud to be a part of the Tree Neutral® program. Tree Neutral offsets the number of trees consumed in the production and printing of this book by taking proactive steps such as planting trees in direct proportion to the number of trees used to print books. To learn more about Tree Neutral, please visit www.treeneutral.com.

Since 1917, Forbes has remained steadfast in its mission to serve as the defining voice of entrepreneurial capitalism. ForbesBooks, launched in 2016 through a partnership with Advantage Media Group, furthers that aim by helping business and thought leaders bring their stories, passion, and knowledge to the forefront in custom books. Opinions expressed by ForbesBooks authors are their own. To be considered for publication, please visit www.forbesbooks.com.

I dedicate this book to my grandmother ("Naani") and my children. Naani, I never had the opportunity to say goodbye. Admittedly, I felt so alone when I was taken to the United States, separated from you. My world became so cold and lonely. I wrestled with the question of why you were taken from me. Now, after having gone through the journey, I know you never left. I see you in other people; I feel you all around me. You're always in my heart. The limited years we had together were the best years of my life, and I owe much of my success to you. You have set an example, for my children and for all of humanity, of what it means to be a loving human being.

To my children, I love each one of you with all my heart. While you are too young to be able to read this now, I wrote this book in the hopes that one day you will pick it up, read it, and apply it to your lives. Perhaps you will gain a better understanding of not only me, but also yourselves. Each one of you was placed on this earth to be special, to make a difference in others. Never be ashamed of who you are; there will never be another person like you, ever. Always do good to others no matter their religion, race, ethnicity, culture, or belief system. Focus on the similarities that unite us, as opposed to the differences that can divide us. Realize that life is tough, filled with challenges and tribulations. At the end, what is important is that you keep moving forward. Be uncompromising in every aspect of your life; never settle for anything less. If you work hard enough and live life through the lenses of love and acceptance, you can have the life you dreamed, no matter what that looks like. Don't stop until you get there. I am, and will always be, proud to be your father.

Contents

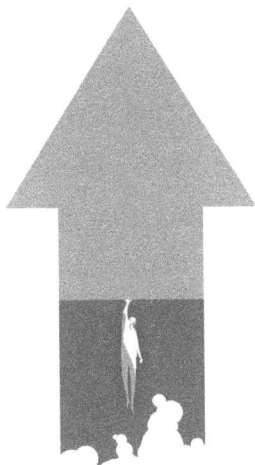

Acknowledgments

WHILE I WAS NEVER handed a business, or anything in life for that matter, I am not "self-made." No person is truly "self-made." We encounter people in our journey that have helped us get to our destination, whether financially, emotionally, through help with resources, or through mentorship. As difficult as my journey has been thus far, it has been the most rewarding due to the amazing people I have met along the way, from my family and friends to random strangers that offered words of encouragement. Thank you—you know who you are. Also, I would like to thank my employees, who work tirelessly for our clients each and every day. We are blessed at ASA to have a team that consists of the most selfless, hardworking individuals in the industry. Special mention to my director of operations, who did not hesitate one second to take the leap with me to help start ASA Law Group—I am forever grateful. Thank you to our clients, whom we have the privilege and honor of serving every day. Thank you for pushing me to reach my potential and for putting your trust not only in myself but also in my team. Last, but certainly not least, thank you to my life partner, who stood with me through one of the toughest chapters of my life. You would not let me give up during or after my divorce, despite every fiber of my being wanting to throw in the towel. Thank you for always being there for me—you are my rock.

The Key Ambition

THIS BOOK TELLS A STORY someone needs to be bold enough to share. It's a story that needs to be told from all sides, because this isn't just about working on matters from a personal or professional end. What I'm about to discuss is an end-to-end approach. No, this is not a self-help book. We're talking about what employees can do on a personal level and what employers can implement at a professional level to create a complete and thorough transformation in people not only for their personal improvement and growth but also for the betterment of companies, their performance, and yes, even their bottom lines. This book is about the ASA Way. In order to fully understand and appreciate the ASA Way, you first need to know me, my story, as it serves as the foundation of the ASA Way. As such, while this book is not an autobiography, it will highlight certain life experiences in a very real, raw fashion. It's time to lace 'em up!

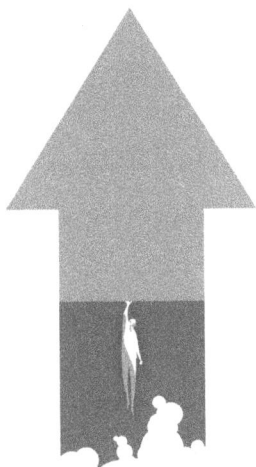

Why?

It's a fair question: Why write this book? And the answer is simple: It's time to wake the hell up. It's time to have an honest conversation about everything going on around us. No filter, no BS—just straight and raw. It's no longer okay to stay quiet and pretend that everything is fine. Because it's not.

The pandemic has pinned our eyes wide open to the truth whether you want to acknowledge it or not, making it more critical than ever to have an honest, candid, cut-to-the-chase dialogue. A dialogue that's way past its stale date. But even with the world tilted sideways on its axis since 2020, people are ignoring the big, fat elephant in the room. They're waltzing past it, limboing under it, stumbling into it day after day only to turn a blind eye to it and proceed with their lives as though nothing has changed, when in fact life's been brought into perspective under a magnifying glass. The world has changed. We've changed. Nothing's the way it used to be. And now more than ever, our home and work lives have practically melded together.

Quarantining at home has meant that all of a sudden, you're no longer pulling out that crisp business suit, slipping into your best-polished shoes, and grabbing a Starbucks from around the bend. You're waking up under a roof that's become your and your family's all-in-one combo of home, office, playground, movie theater, and bar.

People are frustrated as hell. But they're donning a poker face at work, carrying on as though everything is completely normal. Like wearing a shirt or blouse with pajama bottoms is a style that dates back to prehistoric days. Like it's normal to be a quasi–jungle gym for the kids, who are whimpering because they're hungry or don't understand school assignments while you're trying to focus on a Zoom call, acting unfazed. Like it's okay to bottle up the frustrations, because acknowledging or addressing them would mean you're inept or mentally unfit or weak or inferior. So here we are, carrying on and appearing unperturbed, trying to be nothing short of stellar as we struggle—still, in the middle of the madness—to draw a neat line in the sand between our personal and work lives when they've all but become the same damned thing.

As an employer, you have a moral obligation to understand your employees' challenges in the office and outside of it.

If you're an employer, you might be guilty of remaining oblivious to this melee of chaos and its effects. Traditionally, employers are laser focused on the company's bottom line, P&L statements, and growth, making it easy to become tunnel visioned and overlook the obvious. But turning a blind eye to your employees' struggles is outright negligent, especially today. As an employer, you have a moral obligation to understand your employees' challenges in the office and outside of it. That is your job. If you don't think so, then it's time to hang up the cleats and get off the field. The game has changed drastically, and you're about to be left behind.

We've lived through an era, a period that will go down in the books, in which—if it wasn't clear enough before, it should be clear as glass now—it's high time to focus on employees as humans. Acknowledge that these humans are juggling a hell of a lot. Acknowledge that they have lives beyond work that can be challenging, difficult, and nowhere near perfect. Instead of walking around spewing numbers from quarterly reports, pause, get in tune with them, empathize, relate to them, and show them you value them beyond just a means to an end, a bottom-line-boosting resource or a revenue-increasing piece of body mass.

If you're a dollars-and-cents kind of person, here's something to noodle on: embracing this approach will save you money in the long haul better than probably anything else could. For one, it keeps your employees satisfied and feeling empowered. Empowered employees who believe they're genuinely cared for are the best front line to nurturing clients who feel happy and cared for, which increases client satisfaction and boosts revenue.

Second, it's more costly to lose an employee than it is to hire one—and as an employer myself, I can attest to that. Hiring an employee doesn't sap nearly the amount of resources that it does to lose a valued employee you've poured time, energy, resources, and hopes into.

Of course, neither of the above points should be earth-shattering revelations. You've heard it all before, and I'm not here to repeat the obvious. What I am here to say is that now is the time to act. Not just if you're an employee or if you're an employer, but if you're human. This isn't a one-person-does-it-all initiative. It's a side-to-side, end-to-end approach that requires everyone biting the bullet and chipping in.

If you're an employee, it's time to wake up and smell the burnt toast: the one you probably forgot all about while you were juggling twenty other things in this newfound reality. Accept that there's no balancing work and life. Life is work and work is life. Trying to stop one from bleeding into the other is useless and, quite frankly, stupid. You cannot have a successful work life if your personal life is a mess and vice versa. If you are not developing as a person, you will not find sustained success and happiness in your career. Instead you will be going from one job to another thinking that next job will bring you fulfillment. News flash: no one and no external thing will ever bring you fulfillment. Only you can give that to yourself. Realize that the most important person in your life is not your child, not your spouse, not your parents: it's you. And no, that's not being selfish—that is what it takes to be the best version of yourself so that you can live a purposeful life!

And if you're an employer, it's time to foster an environment of care and concern for your employees. Now more than ever, you owe it to them to cut the crap and act beyond the stiff, rigid, traditional boundaries separating employers from employees. Accept them as humans, as people. It's not okay to bury your head in the sand and pretend the new world we live in is a short-term situation that will have no long-term impacts. That when the pandemic lifts, people will automatically become two different people at work and home, with neither drawing any influence from the other. That's never been possible, and it never will be. If anyone has been foolish enough to believe that, it's because they've been hoodwinked by all the Hollywood-worthy acting going on around them. By people unblinkingly sweeping their personal lives under the proverbial rug as best they can, pretending the sharp edges and corners aren't poking and prodding and tearing at them, drawing blood. Because admitting otherwise would be a sign of weakness in an environment and setting in which anything less than perfection is just plain unacceptable and frowned upon.

If you're an employer who actually gives a shit about any of the above, you might find the following question floating through your mind: *How can I invest in an environment where employees feel appreciated and cared for without breaking the bank?*

I'm glad you asked. Because I'm going to walk you through some ideas in the pages to come. One thing working to your advantage is the virtual environment that's come alive as a result of the pandemic. People are more accustomed to navigating technology than before— making it a powerful tool in your arsenal (and saving you serious dollars) as you leverage it to implement the ideas you'll find in this book. A virtual strategy also enables you to reach and empower employees across practically any geographic location. But more to come on that.

So far, everything we've covered probably seems rudimentary, even common sense. That's great. It should, because it is. I haven't revealed any groundbreaking discoveries just yet. Right now, we're simply acknowledging and carrying a dialogue about the obvious— that our personal and professional lives ebb and flow into one another. That when you have a bad day at work, it'll probably come out at home and vice versa.

The problem is that no one is acknowledging the "obvious." And even fewer people are willing to give any thought on how to fix the resulting consequences (more about that momentarily). We could pin the blame, partly, on how we've been conditioned over time, with few, if any, giving thought to the insidious nature of this conditioning or its far-reaching repercussions.

What's Kept Us Pretending

Thinking back to when you were a child, you can probably recall at least a few times you were scolded for being afraid, crying, or feeling upset. Maybe it happened after you got knocked off your bike, sans training wheels, or maybe after you were pummeled by the elementary school bully. Being anything other than strong and composed, even as a child, has been scrutinized through a jaded lens. If you cried, you were slapped with a label: crybaby. If you pouted: cranky pants. If you were sad: downer. These types of reprobation have been engrained in us from the start.

Unfortunately, this mindset is only reinforced as we get older. Once we enter the workforce, we're encouraged—almost forced—to keep personal matters sealed airtight on the other side of office doors. In the process, we're trained to bury our emotions deep beneath the surface, concealing them with a calm composure, as if we're damned robots. The next time you commute to work, look around you, and I bet you'll see this: the commuter uniform—work outfit, headphones, cup of coffee, no eye contact, and heaven forbid a conversation! Robots, that's what we've become.

In fact, think about the word *professionalism*, and you'll realize it's become near synonymous with leaving your personal baggage sealed up at home. And if any of that shit inadvertently tries to sneak out, you're expected to surreptitiously stuff it back in, zip up tight, and toss that damned bag out to sea like flotsam and jetsam. Whether you engage in a full-blown screaming match with your spouse on the way to work or your child throws the granddaddy of all tantrums right before you head out, turning your kitchen upside down and ruining your favorite shirt, you're expected to dig your claws into the dirt and keep going.

And God forbid you make the mistake of airing your personal grievances at the office; you're likely to find yourself, at some point or another, feeling either dismissed or undermined with glib responses like, "Yeah, everybody's got something going on, huh?" or "Think positive" or even "Oh well, life goes on."

If you're a leader eager to run a successful organization, tolerating or embracing this kind of dismissive thinking is toxic to your organization and its staff. Every person is unique—so unique that there can never be an exact replica of that person. There will never be another employee like employee *A*. Recognizing the uniqueness of each individual and fostering a culture where it's acceptable for staff to feel and express emotions so they can process and grow from them is more conducive and beneficial to you and them.

That's exactly where we've gone wrong as a society. Child or adult, we should be able to express our feelings without getting our hands slapped.

It's human to be scared; it's human to cry; it's human to feel sad or have a bad day; it's human to feel.

It's human to be scared; it's human to cry; it's human to feel sad or have a bad day; it's human to *feel*. In fact, the new way of thinking should accept that expressing any emotions is a sign of strength—not weakness. You have to be a stronger, more confident person to express yourself openly, without abandon, than you have to be to bury your emotions deep beneath the surface. Acknowledging those feelings, talking about them, learning from them, and getting better so you're able to manage them is challenging because it requires effort. Ignoring, on the other hand, is something even the unmotivated can accomplish with ease.

How Do We Change the Status Quo? And Why?

Creating a shift in mindset and ideology won't be easy. It's going to require honest, proactive conversations and heavy lifting from people on both ends of the spectrum, from employees to leaders in the workforce. And the conversations can start as early as childhood. For instance, as a parent, I don't tell my kids to tough things out. I tell them it's okay to feel. It's okay to be scared, so long as they're not letting those emotions impede their progress in life. I encourage an open discussion about feelings, asking them questions like, "Are you feeling scared/sad/angry/hurt? Talk to me."

But it doesn't make sense to have parents encourage their kids to be strong individuals who recognize emotions and learn how to express them in healthy ways only for those kids to enter a future workforce where this mindset is discouraged and interpreted as a sign of weakness.

That's why, as I mentioned, this is a dual-level responsibility and message that must be reinforced all the way from employees to leadership-level employers.

What's the point of all this effort? you might wonder. *Why encourage an upheaval from the norm? What's the end result?*

Encouraging this level of acceptance is transformational for everyone involved. Is it challenging to accomplish? Hell yeah. But if it's done correctly, this approach has the potential to build a much healthier dynamic between employers and employees. It can build greater confidence and contentment within people that then ebbs into their attitudes, behaviors, and productivity in the workplace.

From an employer standpoint, encouraging this mindset can be revolutionary. At my law firm, we're seeing exponential growth.

Employees are genuinely happy to come to work, they feel welcomed, they enjoy being with their coworkers, and they know that it's okay to have an off day—that it happens to everyone and anyone who's *human*. It is okay to say, "Today, I am not feeling it." I encourage employees to reach out to each other during those times. I myself periodically text my assistant, saying, "Hey, I need you to keep your eyes on me today. I'm kinda out of it." The workplace must allow this, must encourage it. Without this, we're essentially ignoring the biggest element of what makes us human: love.

If you think about why an approach like this leads to an ideal workplace environment that produces amazing results, it makes sense. Most people spend the majority of their time at work versus home. Think about repressing your feelings and putting on a front during that huge chunk of time, and you can see why phenomena like job stress and anxiety exist in our nation at the staggering levels they do.

For you number lovers, here are some stats to ponder: Approximately 83 percent of workers in the country suffer from work-related stress, which is responsible for 120,000 deaths and results in $190 billion in healthcare costs yearly.[1] Anxiety disorders are the most common mental illness, affecting 40 million adults in the US every year, or 18.1 percent of the population. It's typical for someone with an anxiety disorder to also suffer from depression or vice versa. In fact, nearly half of the people diagnosed with depression are also diagnosed with an anxiety disorder.[2]

Work-related stress can be the pinnacle of anxiety and depression, and this stress can in part stem from feelings of entrapment or from fear of sharing feelings at the risk of being perceived as incompetent

---

1   "42 Worrying Workplace Stress Statistics," The American Institute of Stress, September 25, 2019, https://www.stress.org/42-worrying-workplace-stress-statistics.

2   "Understand Anxiety and Depression: Facts and Statistics," Anxiety & Depression Association of America, accessed April 10, 2021, https://adaa.org/understanding-anxiety/facts-statistics.

or incapable of remaining focused at work. People don't know how much they can safely share with their employers. Is it okay to discuss personal problems? How much sharing is considered too much?

What's worse is that often employees suffering from depression won't seek treatment because they're afraid of the impact it will have on their employment.[3]

This paints a terrifying picture that's entirely unhealthy from an employee standpoint, but it's also one that's shameful from an employer standpoint. If you're an employer who's too stuck in your ways to garner empathy for your employees, they're going to feel rejected. They're going to feel undervalued. They're going to feel unappreciated, and eventually they will leave.

Which brings us back to the Why. The Why of this book is to send a simple message: We don't have to live like this, whether you're an employee or employer. In fact, we damn well shouldn't.

---

3   "Depression in the Workplace," Mental Health America, accessed April 10, 2021, https://adaa.
     org/understanding-anxiety/facts-statistics.

The Awakening

I WAS WORKING my first real job out of law school when it happened.

In law school, I'd specialized in litigation. I lived and breathed and spoke litigation. I'd even attained a litigation certificate, which basically meant I took a hell of a lot of litigation-emphasis classes. Litigation always appealed to me because I love thinking on my feet, I love the mental competition, and most importantly, I love to win.

I say all of this to demonstrate how well versed I was in the courtroom before the incident I'm about to share happened. I was confident in my skin, confident in how to make an ironclad argument, and confident in which tactics to employ to debunk the opposition's points.

There are no doubt many people sharper and more intelligent than me out there, but few can out-prepare me. This case was no different. I knew the parties involved; I knew the case law; I'd even anticipated the arguments from the other side and devised counter rebuttals that could render any potential argument moot. I was ready.

I was rehearsing my notes in my head, going through them repetitively. Finally, our case number was called—it was the opposing counsel's turn to make their points. Sure enough, just as I'd suspected, the attorney argued exactly what I thought he would. Inside, I was smirking. With all my counterpoints laid out, I was, as expected, fully prepared to take it to him—game over, good night!

Then all of a sudden, something strange happened. The opposing council locked gazes with me, started gesticulating, raised his voice to a near holler, and grew theatrical. It was unlike anything I'd ever experienced before and not the way an attorney would argue in a normal professional setting.

For reasons beyond me, his demeanor and countenance triggered something from deep within. I began shaking to the point where I had to force my right hand into my pocket to keep it steady, hoping to make the effect he was having on me less visible to the naked eye.

Ostensibly, I appeared to be listening, maybe even pondering his points, but inside, I was an absolute fucking mess. My heart rate had skyrocketed, and my palms were slick with sweat. I remember asking myself, *What the hell is going on here? This can't have anything to do with his argument. Because the argument this dude is making is not rocket science.*

After the opposing council's five minutes were up, it was my turn. The judge looked at me and nodded, gesturing for me to make my rebuttal. I knew what I had to say. I knew the counterargument. I had it down pat and could recite it with my eyes closed in my sleep. It was all in front of me. But the words would not come out of my throat.

"Mr. Ahmed," the judge said, peering at me from behind the bench. "Please speak up, argue!"

But I couldn't. The words were lodged somewhere between my brain and my tongue in a big, tight knot that refused to unravel and form a coherent stream of thought. The words were literally trapped inside me, unable to scale the insurmountable mountain of dread and fear.

That moment is all it took to change everything: the case, its outcome, and me. The hearing was over almost as quickly as it had begun. The sound of the gavel banging jarred me out of my trance. The decision was rendered: I'd lost.

Shoulders slumped, I gathered my belongings from the courtroom and walked out in a daze, my mind abuzz yet strangely numb at the same time. I had no idea what the hell had just happened. It was the first time ever, in any professional capacity, that I'd felt debilitated, paralyzed, and utterly helpless. I'd let my client down, let myself down.

Reflexively, I pushed past a set of doors as the opposing council sidled up next to me, locking step. "Hey, Shuaib," he said. "What happened back there? Why didn't you say anything?"

I looked at him and shook my head as we shuffled down the lobby. "You know," I said, "I have no fucking clue." And at the time, I didn't. The courtroom had always been my domain. When I was there, I was free. It was a safe haven I felt completely at ease in. I became immersed in the arguments and the defense, my mind becoming part of a universe of its own, shedding all thoughts of anything existing beyond the four walls of the courtroom and the case at hand. Similar to an athlete who draws out the crowd as soon as the game starts.

That day, however, opened my eyes to the fact that something wasn't quite right. There was something deeper at play within me taking rise from a past grievance or event I'd failed to address or lay to rest.

I began digging into it, my curiosity piqued, wondering what was responsible for eliciting this sudden, uncontrolled response so alien to me. I became acutely aware of my reactions after that day, focusing on what triggered each one. On this journey to discovery, I finally figured out what had caused my reaction. Surprisingly, it had everything to do with my past and not much to do with anything that had happened in the present moment, aside, of course, from the triggers of the present that could temporarily immobilize me.

That was a moment of awakening. I realized no matter how passionate I was about law, no matter how swiftly the courtroom swept me into a faraway realm disengaged from the rest of the world, I couldn't escape my past. Our past affects our present and becomes a part of it, no matter where we are physically or how far we come in life. And it doesn't distinguish between which part of our lives it affects—the personal or professional. Because the two aren't separate within us; they're one and the same. If we're one person, how can the feelings and emotions contained within us be segmented and boxed into two disparate parts?

> **Everything you encounter, experience, undergo, withstand, becomes a part of you, a particle of matter that attaches itself to the composition that makes you *you*.**

You're a byproduct, an amalgamation, of everything that's happened to you from the past till this very second. Everything you encounter, experience, undergo, withstand, becomes a part of you, a particle of matter that attaches itself to the composition that makes you *you*. That means the past doesn't magically vanish the moment you set foot in the office; it's already a part of who you are. It bleeds into your present. Obviously, at the time, I didn't know all this. But looking back at my past, I can see now how the events from it came to surface in the middle of those courtroom walls.

PART I

Foundational Elements

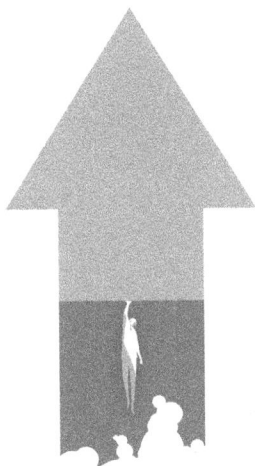

CHAPTER 1

My Story, My Journey

As I MENTIONED in the book's opening, in order to truly understand the principles I share in this book—the ASA Way—you first need to understand me, my journey. This serves as a background to the genesis of my leadership thought. Because I am a lawyer by profession, I thought it only fair to start with a disclaimer:

The viewpoints in this chapter are the author's own. However, it's recognized that, as with any rendition or retelling, incidents can be considered from multiple viewpoints that may at times deviate from one another and often lend deeper clarity into the motivators, triggers, challenges, or emotions of the perspective from which they are told. The incidents shared are not done so maliciously nor to deliver harm, either reputationally or emotionally; rather they are shared for the sole intent and purpose of bringing context to the book and its findings, lending credibility to the book's overall premise and the resulting approach (the ASA Way) backed by the author. The reader is encouraged to consider and respect cultural, religious, and environmental differences that influenced the attitudes and behaviors of the parties discussed.

Now that we've taken care of that bit of housekeeping, I want to share a very personal part of my life with you: my story.

My parents were first-generation Indians when they migrated to the US. As with most immigrants, the promise of freedom and opportunity lured them from their homeland, tantalizing them with hope for a brighter future. Also like most immigrants, they sacrificed a lot. They worked nonstop, long hours, ensconced in a city whose backdrop couldn't be more different from their homeland. The smooth, clean, paved streets of Chicago were a stark contrast to the bustling, littered, potholed ones of India. And the air wasn't punctuated by the aromas of fried *wadas, dosa,* and *paani puri* served by street vendors, who often donned *lungis* and chewed *paan.* Instead, it was infused with the smell of exhaust fume and the occasional waft of perfume drifting from a passerby.

I wasn't there to experience this foreign land just yet. My parents left the country with my siblings when I was only a few years old, entrusting me to the care of my maternal grandmother and uncle. Over time, my recollection of my parents and siblings grew so faint that they went from feeling like a distant memory to a figment of my imagination to nonexistent. It wasn't long before I came to believe that my grandmother was my mother. By the time I was five, I knew my grandmother, grandfather, and maternal uncle to be my only family. All other vestiges of memory had fled. The four of us lived together in a humble residence with the barest of the bare minimum. Resources were limited—limited electricity, limited money, and limited water. But happiness was abundant.

Every morning, around three or four, well before the first ray of daybreak, I'd rub open my eyes and reach out into the darkness for my grandmother's hand. She'd guide us through the flat—much like an apartment—into the humid, pitch-black dusk, eager to secure water for our family before it ran out from the communal well. My grandmother and I would physically pump the water from the well into various buckets or big pans, then lug them back to our flat, where we'd boil and chill the water to eradicate it of germs and bacteria. That water would be just enough for the four of us to drink, bathe, and cook with for the day.

The process for milk was the same, except it required a trek to the local farm in a line that would hold for hours. Women clad in *saris* and *shalwar kameez* of all colors would populate the endless line, their hair, previously tidy in braids and buns, now mussed and unkempt from disturbed sleep. At their hips or atop their heads, they'd clutch urns, pots, or pans prepared to be filled to the brim. For us, there were no such luxuries as popping into the local grocery store to grab a gallon of milk or standing under a running shower that flowed like a waterfall, abundant and unimpeded. And electricity had a mood of its own, a capricious visitor that stayed a sum total of only a few hours a day—on a good day. We would do all of this, daily, at a time of day when many people in civilized nations wouldn't have even begun rolling over in their beds.

Although I was young, I remember growing up in a war-torn India that was vulnerable to perpetual fights that sparked on a whim between Hindus and Muslims. To keep the peace, the country was put under strict curfew, with soldiers taking to the streets and knocking door-to-door to account for every person. As a kid, it was a terrifying ordeal to experience. One night in particular, the ruckus from below roused my interest. I slid a chair against the large peephole in our home that we called a "window" and peered down onto the street. It was past curfew, and the soldiers were out taking count. All of a sudden, an elderly man came into my line of sight. From his hurried pace, I could tell he was trying to scurry home to avoid the wrath of the soldiers. In that moment, time froze. My gut clenched. I knew something terrifying was about to happen. Sure enough, one of the soldiers spotted the man, retrieved a shotgun, aimed, and shot him square in the back. The man fell to the floor, dead on the spot. It was the first time I saw someone's life taken, and I was only four years old.

As stressful as it was to experience poverty coupled with sociopolitical strife, those years were still, hands down, the best years of my life. We didn't have much, yet I felt I had the world.

My grandmother was a mother to me and very nearly a first father, worthy of every praise to describe a magnanimous human. She was charitable, loving, kind, forgiving, patient, and a living, breathing paragon of what being an incredible human means in every faith, religion, and country.

She fed the poor and treated everyone like an equal, irrespective of their socioeconomic class, religious affiliation, or caste. In fact, she fed the poor first, and we would eat if there was anything left over. She always reminded me that if you took care of others, God would take care of you. She was devoutly religious, always praying and encouraging me to pray my problems away. She had a loving manner and the most patience I've ever seen a human possess. And she was selfless beyond measure. Yet despite the exemplary human being she was, her relationship with my grandfather wasn't what she deserved. He was an absent husband and an angry one, from what I remember. He'd often yell, curse, or pitch a fit for no reason apparent to anyone, taking advantage of my grandmother's perpetual kindness. But no matter how ugly he got, my grandmother not once ever retaliated.

She remained calm, kind, and quiet despite being constantly berated, ridiculed, disrespected, and insulted. Many times, I would ask her why she didn't respond to his antics. Was it because she was afraid of him? She would answer with a smile and simply say that as humans, we have no right to judge anyone, because we cannot know or fully comprehend the struggles of others.

Her warm nature and unconditional love set a solid example of what it meant to be a respectable person and were instrumental in shaping who I became. As a young boy, I thrived under her watch, growing well rounded in every aspect of life, be it sports, social circles, or school, where I excelled, making top-of-class grades and being placed under consideration to skip a grade, which was a huge deal.

My grandmother's presence brought me such happiness, love, and a sense of belonging that it obliterated from view the material shortcomings in our lives. For a long time, that was the last place I associated with feeling safe. The values she practiced and taught, many of which I share in this book, grew deeply embedded in me throughout my childhood. Later, I'd learn those values are the very ones some of the best leaders in business swear by today.

My maternal uncle was a fatherlike figure for me as a child. Apart from my parents, this man was the single most hardworking person I'd ever met. He would leave early morning and return well after dark from the travel agency he owned next to our home. All day I'd hang out at his office, observing his work, how he communicated with people, and the way he went about his business. I sat in on every meeting, phone conference, and discussion, watching him interact in his jolly way as he made people feel important and cared for and showed a genuine interest in their well-being. During many of our talks throughout the day, he'd advise me on the art of connecting with people. Money is nice, he would tell me, but the real prizes are the relationships you build.

Overall, life as I knew it at the time was perfect. And then it turned upside down.

I was nearly seven when I returned home to see two strangers in our small flat. I'd never once laid eyes on this pair before: a man and a woman. Instinctively, I sidled toward my grandmother, keeping my gaze on them. She hugged me close and introduced the woman in her quiet, kind manner.

"This is your mother," she told me. I stared at the woman in front of me and then up at my grandmother, disbelieving. If I didn't know any better, I would have thought she was playing a cruel joke on me, because to me, the woman holding me was my mother, so the words coming out of her mouth baffled me, making no sense. How could that woman be my mother when as far back as I could remember, I'd lived with this mother?

At my shocked silence, she continued, explaining that these strangers would take me to a different country. When I looked up at her questioningly, my thoughts still muddled, she held me close and explained that I'd be leaving soon and that the move would be permanent.

I will never in my life forget the ride to the airport. I was miserable, sad, and terrified. At the time, planes were boarded from outside the gate, and you'd climb up a ramp to enter the plane. As it was time to exit the double doors that led outside, I remember hanging on to my uncle's leg, begging and crying for him not to let me go. The tears swam into my nose and mouth and dribbled down my chin as I pleaded for him to not put me on that plane, my words stumbling over each other and running together, incomprehensible to even my own ears.

Even then, a part of me sensed that crossing through those double doors would lead me from a place where I felt implicitly safe, loved, and happy to someplace portentous and different from anything I'd ever known. The plane itself, to me, represented an ominous, massive turning point in my life. A place of no return.

As we boarded the plane, a single thought kept playing through my mind on repeat: there's no way I'm going back. As fast as my legs would carry, I scurried to the window seat, tears of grief and betrayal streaming down my face. I couldn't understand why the people I'd loved so dearly would do such a thing to me. Maybe I'd done something wrong? Maybe they'd decided they'd had enough of me? Maybe they'd never truly loved me? My mind was an abyss of questions that had no sensible answers.

As the doors to the plane closed and we started taxiing away, my hands splayed across the small window. My eyes remained on my naani and uncle until they were tiny specks, and then we turned the bend and they disappeared.

Grief swallowed me whole every time I woke up only to realize that what happened wasn't a nightmare—I was living the nightmare.

The flight was long, and I was in and out of sleep, exhausted from heartache. Grief swallowed me whole every time I woke up only to realize that what happened wasn't a nightmare—I was living the nightmare.

In America, I met my three siblings for what I could recall was the first time. I quickly learned that my parents worked like demons. They didn't know much English, didn't have much money, and didn't know anyone around. Basically, they were building their lives, and ours, from the ground up in every aspect imaginable.

As first-generation Indians in this country, they still held fast to the culture and norms of their homeland. A country where sloppy work, a disheveled appearance, or even incorrect answers in school were rewarded with a slap to the wrist with a ruler, often leaving an imprint for days. Aunts and uncles held liberty to spank you for misdemeanors like back talk or mischief. Chiding, hitting, and raising kids authoritarian-style were very much part of the norm in most, though not all, households across the country. But what was the norm for many in a country of over seven hundred million was not the norm for me. My grandmother hadn't raised me that way. Her approach to child-rearing was ahead of her time—she was an anomaly.

I remember being slapped for the first time in my life after I moved with my parents to the US. I remember the immediate, reflexive sting of tears, the ringing in my ears, and feeling a moment of dizziness and the shame of humiliation. Until then, nobody had ever laid a hand on me.

Anytime my grandmother had been angry or upset, she never raised her hands or voice. Instead she treated me to something far more lethal: her silence. That silence was enough to make me squirm, sweat, and feel so uneasy I wanted to cry. At times I'd wished she'd just slap me instead.

But my dad was a disciplinarian, a no-nonsense businessman, and a hustler. He believed in hard work and the notion that there was no time in life for complaining, feeling sorry for yourself, or making excuses. At one point, he was managing four businesses single handedly. Often he would return home from work well after we'd fallen asleep. Perhaps the thing that stood out to me most about him was how he was rigid, almost emotionless. I recall being with him one day as he worked under the hood of his car. When he was done, he slammed the hood shut on top of my fingers. I hollered in pain.

He took one look at me, opened the hood, and simply walked away, leaving me to stare at four bloodied fingers that I could have sworn were broken. I never remember having any father-son conversations with him. Instead ours was a relationship of obligation: as long as I did my chores and homework and stayed out of his way, we were fine.

In spite of being raised in a war-torn and poverty-stricken country and witnessing homicide, I felt levels of anxiety and fear after migrating here that were incomparable to anything I'd ever experienced. With every passing year, the scars of discipline worsened, commensurate with my sense of fear, dread, and resentment.

One day, after school, when I was in the second or third grade, a teacher greeted me in the hallway. "You had a really great day in class today," he said.

I thanked him, shuffling my feet while glowing with pride and embarrassment.

"I'm really proud of you," he said, and he gave me a pat on the back.

I screamed.

The teacher jumped, startled. He asked what was wrong, a look of concern clouding his face.

I told him nothing, that I was fine. But his dubious expression told me he didn't believe me.

"Mind if I take a look at your back?" he asked.

I nodded, my years of training from India to respect and defer to teachers kicking in automatically. Fear snaked through me at what I knew he'd find. After a moment of silence, he asked me how I'd managed to bruise my back.

"I climbed a tree and fell," I said.

The teacher frowned. "Are you scared?" he asked. "Anything happening at home?"

I shook my head vehemently. Days later, a few officious-looking people showed up at our front door. Part of me was terrified as I learned what they were there for. The other part was hoping, almost praying, that this would put a stop to the endless fear. The people came in, spoke with my parents, and left. After that day, I never saw the strangers again.

I remember feeling helpless and crestfallen. I'd really been pinning my hopes on those strangers, hoping they'd be the answer to the pain.

Of course, at the time there was no education on the impact of physical violence on children. And my parents, I know now, weren't trying to be malicious or abusive. They were simply following the norm by embracing a form of punishment that was acceptable in their generation and country.

They were also God-fearing, devout Muslims. Growing up, I was taught to pray and read the Quran. And if my siblings or I didn't, we were punished. Also, if we didn't stand a certain way in prayer or recite things accurately, we were punished. And punishment meant physical abuse. The most God-loving person I knew, my grandmother, had never resorted to such tactics. With her I'd enjoyed and respected religion. But now religion went from being an admirable practice to a dreaded one that elicited fear of brutality. I began to derive a very convoluted picture of religion, and in time, I decided I wanted nothing to do with it.

What I was told to be in terms of my religion and culture were the exact things I began to despise being. The people I was exposed to from my culture and religion never seemed accepting of anything outside of it. The restrictions, the limitations, the judgment—all of it suffocated me. I felt like I couldn't breathe.

By the time I was in the sixth grade, matters at home only worsened. I started fantasizing about running away. I would stay up at night game-planning different strategies to execute my getaway plans. I was defeated, exhausted, and still scared. And I was tired of living in fear.

Each time the school bus inched toward my house, my hands would start shaking and I'd sweat profusely, never knowing what was waiting inside that front door. I would pray nobody was home. As the bus made the final turn, my eyes would dart to the driveway, and I dreaded to see which vehicles, if any, were parked outside. My heart would pound, and a knot would settle itself in my stomach. It would feel like my insides were about to spill out.

Each day when that bus rolled to a screeching halt, I was never ready to get off. Unlike the other kids antsy to get home, I would have willingly stayed on all day, appreciating the safe harbor. Often I wished there was another place the bus could take me, any place except home.

The trek to the front door was often the most difficult part of my journey each day. I'd drag my feet, my heart in my throat, stomach in knots, walking as slowly as I possibly could. Once inside, my ears would perk up, growing attuned to the smallest sounds. If I saw anyone, I'd immediately gauge their body language, facial expressions, and stance to get a sense of their mood. Then I'd scamper up the stairs as fast as I could, stumbling over my feet until I was behind the sanctity of my room door. Only then would I breathe easy, unwilling to come out unless beckoned or required. I'd gone from a free-spirited child playing soccer in the dingy streets of India to a kid who hid in his room and never wanted to leave. There were times I would stay in there so long my stomach would growl in protest, but I was too afraid to walk the fifteen paces to the kitchen. I didn't know what would transpire in those fifteen steps or what fate would befall me. So I stayed in my room until I fell asleep, the rumblings of my stomach becoming a familiar lullaby. I preferred to face moments of hunger than moments of fear.

By the time I was in eighth grade, my prayer every night would be to not wake up in this world. And every time I opened my eyes, I hated God. I hated him for keeping me alive. Hated him for putting me through this pain. I was a child ... what did I do to deserve this? The pain was too much to bear, and not living would mean the end to that pain. To stay away from home, I took up sports in high school, channeling all my energy into them and thriving. I played competitive sports all year round and spent numerous hours perfecting my skills along with my brothers. Sports brought my brothers and I together. But whatever I immersed myself in, I made sure to steer clear of the Indian culture and its people, my mistrust of them deeply seated.

> **It felt like I was operating in survival mode at all times, constantly suppressing my wants against what was expected of me so that I could adhere to the cookie-cutter perfect life I was supposed to be living.**

Making friends with Indians gave me anxiety, so all of my friends were non-Indians, except for one in particular whom I felt I could confide in completely. He was an outcast of sorts, one of the few who dared to date outside our culture. Maybe what drew him to me was his boldly rebellious courageousness—because for me, doing something like that would have been equivalent to a death sentence. It felt like I was operating in survival mode at all times, constantly suppressing my wants against what was expected of me so that I could adhere to the cookie-cutter perfect life I was supposed to be living.

When it was time to attend college, I was accepted into Creighton University in Omaha, a Jesuit college. As I came from a staunch Muslim family, the irony of that didn't escape me.

College almost took my life, but ultimately it also saved it. The sentiments I experienced my first time on campus juxtaposed perfectly with the sentiments I'd experienced boarding the flight to the US all those years ago, one antithetical to the other. Where there was anguish before, there was elation now. Where there was hopelessness before, there was hope now. The only fine line of similarity running parallel between both instances was the thought running on repeat through my mind, just as it had back then: there's no way I'm going back. This time, however, it was repeated with fierce will and determination.

It didn't take long for me to realize I was happiest away from home. I felt relieved, free, alive.

The experiences I had and the people I met—people from all cultures, religions and walks of life—gave me new hope that there could be a better tomorrow for me. Still, I found myself shrinking away from people of my own culture and religion.

While I retreated from my own religion, I grew to accept a broader belief system. I started attending a multifaith candlelight "mass" on campus every Sunday evening. Even though it couldn't be categorized as a religion per se, the mass was such a refreshing take on what I believe religion should be: listening to sermons, talking about hope, and cultivating acceptance. This resonated so much better with me than the sermons I'd grown up with, during which I felt threatened with punishment at every corner of perceived failure. I'd come to think of God as this angry man who created a bunch of human beings only to smack his head in frustration when he realized he'd created some really horrible people. But this, what I was experiencing, went against all those beliefs. Here I found a sense of peace and calm in thoughts of God. I started becoming close to God and had started talking to him regularly. Here he was merciful, kind, benevolent. Everything my grandmother had reinforced from the beginning.

Slowly I began to heal. Slowly I started to let go.

The assistant dean of students at the university, Dr. Tanya Winegard, was the first person with whom I ever broke my silence. She would sit with me for hours, talking through years of bottled-up emotions and incidents. For the first time in my life, a huge burden lifted from my shoulders; I finally had an adult figure in my life whom I could talk to freely for the first time since my grandmother. The people around me were open minded, loving, and accepting—a completely new experience for me that felt indescribably refreshing. My roommate—who was a man of faith and didn't drink or party much, like other college kids—became like a brother to me. In fact his father took me to my very first NFL game at Mile High Stadium. While I was there, I felt I finally had permission to be who I was without fear of retaliation.

Eventually I started dating. One of my brothers also attended the same university, which meant I had to keep my relationships mum, being cognizant about who knew about them and where we went. I was taught that to date was to go against not only our culture but also our religion, as though loving someone was a sin and choosing to share a life with someone outside my culture and religion was blasphemous. Shame, guilt, and fear became my everyday emotions as I discovered relationships. But even as I began dating these women, all of whom were incredible people, I found myself clamming up, unable to fully connect to any of them. Something inside me just wouldn't allow it.

They would take me home to meet their families, who were generous enough to treat me like one of their own, showering me with love and compassion. The family dynamics I witnessed were in stark contrast to my own understanding of how families functioned, which was pretty violent. I continually asked myself, How can this much love, this much graciousness, be a sin? Is God against love?

Instantly I began to long for their acceptance and love and for the safety I felt in their homes. And then the inevitable happened: word got around to my parents that I was dating. The news was treated with fury and disdain, the equivalent of committing a crime worthy of *The Scarlet Letter*. In hindsight, it seems ridiculous. But in the moment, I remember the intense fear, anguish, and dread. My father demanded a discussion, and he finished with an ultimatum: either I stopped dating, and they'd continue to support me financially with my student loans; or I could do whatever I wanted, and they'd cut me loose from the financial assistance and the family. Those choices presented a defining moment for me. Here I was, an adult who could finally choose to give way for my inner voice, honor it, and be true to it, or do what I'd always been forced to: suppress it, be the obedient son, and acquiesce to the life my parents had decreed for me. Right then, I knew that if I wanted a different life, I had to be brave enough to take a different path. So I chose to break free. To be fair, I'll admit that if I'd been home, face-to-face with my parents, I probably would have never been bold enough to make that decision. However, the distance afforded by a telephone line made it easier. To make ends meet and pay tuition, I took on a few jobs. But it was challenging. Most months I could barely make tuition, and most days my meals could barely be classified as such. Dinner often looked like cheese slices melted over rice with ketchup. I took on pretty much every job imaginable, from lawn mowing to serving tables to working as a bellman and every job in between.

I went from feeling like I could win in college to feeling helpless and hopeless all over again. There were times life became so unbearable I wanted to give up on it altogether. Bring a permanent end to the misery. With the number of hours I worked, I could barely make enough to keep a roof over my head, and I couldn't get rid of the blisters from my feet or the exhaustion from my legs, let alone appease the constant growling in my tummy.

I'd attempted suicide a few times in high school and then again that year in college, going to the busiest street in Omaha, centric to shopping malls and traffic.

There, in the middle of the intersection, at 2:42 a.m., I laid down. I could feel the ice-cold road on my back as I looked up at the dark, smoggy clouds. I remember telling myself that in no time, I will be set free. Free from the pain, free from the shame, free from the fear. I closed my eyes for what I was convinced would be the last time. Just as I did, a truck barreled toward me, closer and closer. But then, like the previous times, a voice in my head whispered frantically. This time it was urging me to get up, get up, get up, get up!

I missed the truck by a breath, feeling the wind snap by me, the driver honking up a furious storm as it whizzed by.

At the time, I had no idea my grandmother had passed away a few years back. No one told me until my later years in college. My brother was the last person to see her, and her final words to him were to "look after Shuaib." Now, thinking back, it makes more sense: I believe the voice in my mind always ushering me away from self-harm was my grandmother's.

After that incident, something in me changed. I was determined to remain undeterred in completing college, even if I had to do it all on my own. I had very little—really close to nothing. In fact those days reminded me so much of my days growing up in India, having barely any money ever. But like in India, even with very little, I was still okay. As long as I had the necessities, I felt fortunate.

Some days I didn't have enough to make bills; others I didn't have enough to fill gas in my car. One such time, I was working for a hotel in Omaha and had to make the two-hour trek to work by foot. I needed the money desperately, but I was determined to pave my own path, be true to myself, break free from the shackles of violence that had consumed my childhood. Going back to being under my parents' control was never an option in my mind.

With finances a constant distraction, my grades faltered. I went from being a good student to one on the verge of failing out. Fortunately, I had amazing friends and teachers who showed up miraculously each and every time the going got tough. My friends' parents stepped in to loan me money so I could stay in school, offering me comfort and giving me a sense of belonging. Many of the ones who reached out to lend a helping hand were from outside of my own culture and religion. They opened their homes and hearts to me for Christmas and gave me a place at the table on Thanksgiving. This was such a huge shift from what I was used to and opened my eyes to the goodness in people. The experience taught me that there was another side to life that had nothing to do with anger and fear and animosity. My professors, in particular my marketing professor at Creighton University, sat me down after class and said, "Shuaib, you are better than this. You are too talented to allow yourself not to succeed." Those words would echo in my mind for years to come. These people, whom I barely knew, had quite literally rescued me, sometimes in the form of a loan, sometimes with a meal, sometimes with a smile or a handshake. They were angels. And some way, somehow, they always showed up to support me right when I needed it most.

By the time I was a junior in college, I'd made progress in healing and decided it was time to make peace with my family and the past. My parents and I didn't have to agree on everything, I knew. But maybe in spite of our differences, we could still maintain some semblance of a relationship. Going back was terrifying. But I went on principle: my parents were still my parents and, as dysfunctional as we may have been, we were still a family. That said, I forgave them not for them, but for me. I knew that the only way for me to make progress was to release the burden of those emotions, which started with forgiveness. From that point, in my mind, any setback I'd experienced merely set the stage from where I'd make my greatest comeback.

I began applying to law school around then, attracted to justice and the ability to help those who couldn't help themselves. Perhaps a part of it was that I'd wished there had been someone for me growing up, lawyer or not, who could have intervened and helped me.

By then, however, my grades had taken a serious beating, and I received rejection letters from twenty-two of the twenty-three colleges I'd applied to—letters I still keep to this day. A poor GPA, as it turned out, made it extremely challenging to get into law school.

The one school in Michigan that accepted me did so on a conditional basis—if I didn't flunk out, I could stay. This only strengthened my resolve, and I became eager to prove myself. With amazing professors and my determination fueling me, I did well, and my confidence level started rising again. I got into litigation pretty heavily and did exceptionally well with it. But the ghosts of the past still haunted me.

At night I'd find myself writhing in my sleep or unable to close my eyes as hour upon waking hour I relived the past. The rare nights I did find sleep, I hated waking up in the morning to catch sight of myself in the mirror. The nail marks etched in my face were an unwelcome specter lingering in my life—a permanent, unflinching reminder of incidents I'd rather have forgotten. Despite my achievements in law school, I couldn't escape. Yelling, screaming, intimidation—all paralyzed my mind. Here we go again, it would warn me. And that's exactly what triggered my debilitation that day in the courtroom.

As a lawyer, I felt horrible that day. I'd let my clients down, let myself down. I knew there was something bigger at play that I wasn't fully grasping. I recall sitting down on the court steps, the winter wind whipping around me. My face was freezing. But I felt the heat of humiliation like fire in my veins.

That was my first true encounter with my personal life affecting my professional one. I'd always seen the two as distinct, disparate from each other. This was implied in school and the many jobs I had held in the professional world. Like many people, I'd fallen for the hype that there was a way to neatly define and separate each: here's my personal life, and here's my professional one. But here I was, unable to draw that line.

Everything from my past had shaped who I'd become as an individual, as a person, and as a professional. From my grandmother and those early years under her care to my adolescent and adulthood years in the US, there was no single aspect that defined who I

And the more I acknowledged the complexities that made me *me*, the better I could manage myself and how I thrived both personally and professionally. I learned that's true of anyone. We are the sum of our parts.

was—I was and am a combination of all my experiences throughout the years. I'm the boy who played soccer in the mud and the same one who wouldn't leave his room. The one who laughed freely and also the one who forgot how to laugh. And the more I acknowledged the complexities that made me *me*, the better I could manage myself and how I thrived both personally and professionally. I learned that's true of anyone. We are the sum of our parts.

This discovery led me to use my findings and personal experiences to explore an approach I thought could help not only me but also others.

I call this approach the ASA Way, and it started as a concept I wanted to implement to help others thrive in their personal lives, which would then bleed into their professional lives. Today, it's a proven success story evident through both me and my employees, and one I wanted to share with as many people as I could, because it's life altering.

But before we delve into the ASA Way and how it works, we're going to cover ground on another really important chapter that addresses a critical topic—embracing the right mindset.

CHAPTER 2

Getting Your Shi(f)t Together

YOU MIGHT ASSUME LIFE CHANGED drastically for me after I came to terms with my parents. In some ways it did, and in many ways it didn't. I loved them like hell, and they loved me. Yet at every turn, I found myself in a tug-of-war between who they wanted me to be and who I really was—two identities that couldn't have been more in contrast and at odds with each other.

For the longest time, I felt there was something seriously wrong with me. Why didn't I have any Indian friends? Why did my heart feel like jumping out of my throat anytime I went to a mosque? My siblings were conforming to the cultural expectations so well, acceding to arranged marriages without batting an eyelash, following the rules and being obedient in every way possible. I was the only misfit.

Throughout college, I grew close to people outside my culture, dated outside my culture, and lived with families from outside my culture and religion. And then all of a sudden, to appease my parents and secure acceptance from family, I found myself considering an arranged marriage—a notion so far out of left field it was the perfect contradiction to everything that defined me. Culturally, marrying someone who is educated, has a solid career, and hails from a good family (the logic being that the apple doesn't fall far from the tree) is the norm. And if you're lucky as hell, love (if it ever happens) comes later. This was my chance at giving my parents the redemption I felt I owed, a way to somehow make amends and right my wrongs. After years of being the black sheep of the family, severed from my parents, my inner child was begging for acceptance, approval, and belonging, and I was confident this was my way back in. Also, the girl's family treated me with respect, were accomplished, and checked all the cultural boxes.

By then I'd already resigned myself to the fact that marrying someone outside the culture just wasn't going to happen. Subjecting them to a closed-minded mentality where they'd never feel fully embraced, loved, or appreciated would have been not only unfair and unjust to them but also selfish on my part.

I figured I'd try to make the arranged marriage setup work, and I gave the nod to my parents, who never technically forced me into the marriage. At the end, acceptance had been fully my decision. Some of my family members and those who knew me well were flabbergasted, to say the least. "What the hell are you doing, Shuaib?" my cousins asked me. But I was hell bent on going forth with the wedding, convinced this was the right thing.

Of course, looking back, I would have done things differently had I felt I had permission and courage to safely claim me for who I was. Given I was married into a culture and religion that brought me so much pain growing up, the triggers in the marriage were overwhelming at times. I wanted to break free from this shackle of dysfunction. Just when I thought it was behind me, here it was rearing its ugly head in my marriage and, worse, in front of my children. Something had to give, and it did. At the time, I didn't fully understand what the hell type of a dilemma I was creating for myself and everyone involved or how badly I was about to fuck everyone's lives over. It turned out that settling for an arranged marriage would be equally as damaging to everyone involved as me bringing someone from outside the culture into my family would have been—if not more.

I'd never been the guy who believed in the cultural and religious norms and rules engrained in me from the time I was young. I'd found that the people who followed these rules to a *T* were often the most miserable, angry people I'd ever met in my life. Let's be clear—I am not saying that all people who follow a certain religion or culture are not genuinely happy. What I'm saying is during my lifetime, I've met very few of them. Yet I caved into the expectations. It was important to my ex-wife that I didn't drink at client engagements and that I follow the rest of our cultural, societal, and religious cues. Soon I realized that everyone in my life had become more important than me. I didn't drink because of my then wife. I came to the mosque because of my parents. I didn't do something else because it would offend this person or that person. In the process, I started losing myself. It was almost like there were two different mes. I was leading a double life: one outwardly and one inside my mind, where I was yearning to be me. My inner voice was bellowing that I was an imposter, that I was inauthentic, that I was a liar, lying to myself. While I won't go into details, the divorce involved a lot of heartache and was unfair to everyone involved. My family didn't deserve the cultural humiliation. My kids didn't deserve to feel like they had to choose between Mommy or Daddy, told their father was responsible for breaking up the family—a terrible person who they shouldn't follow. My ex-in-laws did not deserve the perceived betrayal. My clients did not deserve being pulled into litigation by way of subpoenas that, in my opinion, were baseless and solely aimed at destroying my livelihood. I did not deserve to be publicly shamed, embarrassed, labeled as a dishonorable person. That moment in my life was my moment of realization. It made me realize the importance of being authentic and true to myself.

In any society, culture, or country, we're taught that living a certain way and abiding to certain expectations is the right thing to do. That's bullshit. The right thing to do is what you believe is the right thing to do. And sometimes that requires a hell of a lot of courage, because you might sit alone in your beliefs. But the alternative—creating a life where your actions are disjointed from who you are—will create innumerable challenges that can carry ugly repercussions, sometimes, as in my case, impacting even innocent people associated with each party.

That's why this chapter on authenticity is crucial. Consider this chapter the primer to the rest of the book, like the stuff professional painters apply before they roll on the paint. Without this foundation, the results this book will help you achieve will be limited, maybe even abysmal. Because the greatest power you have is your mind—and without first priming it, just like you would with paint, you won't get optimal results.

So let's start there and get to work on prepping your mind.

This book requires you to accept a few hard truths that you may initially find difficult to swallow, only because our minds have been conditioned to accept what's antithetical to these truths. First, shun the previous doctrines that say you have to be a different person at work and another at home. No, you don't. Look in the mirror. You're one person, not two. Expecting anything different of yourself is not only attempting to defy the laws of nature but is also flat-out delusional thinking.

Second, accept that because you are one person with one mind, your personal life will bleed into your professional one. That's not by choice. It's just natural. You can't be in a professional setting and tune out or turn off what's happening in your personal life, what is happening inside your head. Expecting that is plain futile and senseless.

Last, and perhaps most importantly, learn from my mistakes and accept authenticity as the norm. Stop being a robot and automatically giving in to what's expected of you. Be proud

> **Be proud of being authentically you. There will never be another you, ever.**

of being authentically you. There will never be another you, ever. What does that say? That you are unique, were created to be different, were created to be special. We just need to start living that way.

Let's look closer at each of these three points or, as I like to call them, mindset shifts.

Mindset Shift #1: Stop Playing Jekyll and Hyde

Imagine being a different person behind closed doors at home. Then imagine having to be a different person at your place of business. In front of your friends. In front of your parents. In front of your kids.

You're probably not having to work hard at imagining; this is the reality for most people.

For as far back as we can remember, the notion of behaving in different ways around different people has been engrained into our minds as traditional practice. You have to be smart, intelligent, on your A game at work. Patient, understanding, and the ideal role model in front of your kids. And fun, kind, and present with your friends. In fact being able to be all these different personalities is actually viewed as an admirable "skill." Guess what? It's not. Why? Because doing that takes no courage. None. All you have to do is conform to a system that is already in place, formed by societal, familial, or cultural norms. All you're doing is playing your role. That's easy. There's nothing admirable or special about it. By comparison, going against the norms, being one person at all times regardless of the situation, people, atmosphere, role, etc.—that takes courage. That requires you to regularly break those norms and be completely confident, secure, and free.

The real you probably exists somewhere in the middle of all the different personas you take on every day. But there's only one true you. And that means the things you struggle with or that trigger a certain reaction in your personal life are also going to provoke a similar reaction in your professional life. If there's an attitude or behavior that irks you at home, it's likely to have the same effect in the workplace, no matter how hard you try to hide beneath layers of professionalism and diplomacy. Recall my episode in the courtroom I referenced toward the beginning of this book. You can attempt to proactively control your emotions or thoughts, but the fact that it's there, requiring control, tells you it's a part of you—and there's absolutely nothing wrong with that. Because you're not two different people. You're one.

For employees, however, extricating themselves from the mindset of associating different identities of themselves with different crowds is a deeply rooted notion. Often when I speak with people, I'll hear things like, "Well, Shuaib, what you're expecting is just a tough way to think." Or they'll ooze confidence and say, "I don't think like that. I tell myself, 'This is my professional self, and this is my personal self.' I'm pretty good at keeping both parts of me separate."

My answer to them is *No, you're not, because if you were, you probably would be well ahead of where you are now.* A part of the struggle for both employers and employees is this: How do we align these two parts of our lives? Because more times than not, they're totally out of sync with each other, leading to dissatisfaction and an internal crisis. That's why people do inexplicable things, like perpetually job hop, thinking that if they accept a certain role or work for a specific company, they'll find satisfaction. They look externally for what's internal, within their reach—because satisfaction lies inside you. It comes when you're one within yourself, not when you're trying to reconcile ten different personas into one you.

A part of the mindset shift is to acknowledge that satisfaction is derived from within and to progress in such a way that allows us to be the best version of ourselves each and every day, regardless of which platform we're on: whether you're Jane the employee/employer or you're Jane the parent, spouse, sibling, or friend.

And as an employer, you should acknowledge the value in your workers and employees being uniquely themselves. Accepting and respecting each individual exactly as he or she is should

Accepting and respecting each individual exactly as he or she is should be an organic part of your company culture.

be an organic part of your company culture, a topic we'll delve into a bit more later.

The beauty of it is that this mindset shift isn't something that should happen at one level of the organization or another. To be truly effective, this mindset must be accepted from the individual level all the way up to the organizational level and every place in between.

Mindset Shift #2: Stop Trying to Draw a Line between Personal and Professional

What's ridiculous is that after experiencing a pandemic, when employers should be more attuned than ever to their employees' sentiments and well-being, some couldn't be more oblivious or intentional in suppressing the reflexive care and concern that should be a natural reaction to our circumstances. Instead they're too busy fighting to cling to old-school ideologies that tout the separation of work from home, almost tripping over themselves as they attempt to halt the collision of these two worlds—all because of a dated taboo forbidding the two to ever intersect. If you don't believe me, think of the first thing you do when you're getting ready to join a Zoom call. You line up babysitting and make sure your workspace looks spotless (and like an actual workspace). And if it doesn't, you have these magnificent virtual backgrounds that plop you in front of the Golden Gate Bridge or on a beach in the Maldives, giving you a picturesque backdrop that at the same time conceals the imperfections of your real life (like the damned laundry basked that hasn't budged or the treadmill that's been repurposed to a coatrack).

But living like this isn't realistic, and it's a disservice for you to constantly feel like you need to be nothing short of perfect—even in choosing which damned corner of the house you work from.

Sure, things have changed a bit. Now when you attend Zoom calls, you might catch sight of your coworkers' kids or their pets prancing around like they own the place, and you hear meowing or barking more often than you hear your coworker speaking. This is great.

When any of this happens, I make it a point to tell people who feel nervous that it's okay for all of the above to happen—it just proves they're humans who have lives outside of work. But now it feels like we're almost trying to revert back to how life used to be pre-pandemic, bury the past year and a half deep in a ditch, and carry on as if it was a blip in time that never happened.

At the company level, you hear rumblings of impatience among leaders and executives who have grown weary of their own benevolence and "generosity" over the course of the pandemic and now frown upon these "intrusions." *We've been in COVID-19 for a year,* they say, *Haven't you figured out babysitting yet?* Or, *by now you've had enough time to sort out whatever adjustments you needed to make.* This is fucked up. Instead the conversation should start with, *How can we help you? Are you feeling overwhelmed?*

Even better would be to provide resources or flexibility to accommodate associates in whatever environment or situation they find themselves in.

A mindset shift embracing that the personal and professional are interconnected—and that this is the new norm—is critical. These mindset shifts, however, cannot simply take place at the employee level, where employees acknowledge the overlapping of these aspects of their lives. It must also be a change present in employers' minds, attitudes, and behaviors, which we'll address more deeply in a later chapter.

Mindset Shift #3: Be True to You

If we had to pin a definition to authenticity, it would be this: being completely honest with yourself and free of judgment or shame about who you are and what you stand for. An indication of true authenticity is an individual whose internal reflects their external and external reflects their internal.

You don't and shouldn't fit in a box or conform to a specific blueprint. You're your own blueprint. Embrace that, because it's a blessing. There's nothing wrong with you believing in things others don't. There's nothing wrong with you feeling strongly about matters others suppress a yawn at. The most important thing that matters is being brutally honest with yourself.

Being authentic is not always as simple as it sounds. But once you get there, I can tell you it's the most liberating feeling in the world. You accept who you are, and you're comfortable in your skin and what you stand for. You understand your values and life vision; and in that, you find your true purpose.

There's no cookie-cutter employee; each person, employee or not, is unique and comes with their own flaws, attributes, and idiosyncrasies.

From an organizational perspective, authenticity means embracing employees for who they are without expecting them to smother their inner selves. Anticipating that employees will muffle their true identities or chuck them out the door makes for an inattentive, inauthentic company in and of itself. In fact, the very notion of expecting people to magically transform into model employees who meet your every expectation is old school and dated. There's no cookie-cutter employee; each person, employee or not, is unique and comes with their own flaws, attributes, and idiosyncrasies.

From an employee perspective, this mindset shift requires you to shed any facades and arrive at work unapologetic, unafraid, and unencumbered with who you think you're expected to be. And that's where the mindset shift must start: with you. You being not just authentic but more importantly understanding that it's okay to be different. If you believe you're already authentic, take a moment to analyze what you do and why you do it. Do you 100 percent believe in everything you do and say? Chances are you don't. Chances are sometimes you do something not because you believe or see value in it but because you're trying hard to appease someone else.

In the process, you'll do like I did and lose a piece of yourself, or all of yourself. You cannot be two different people personally and professionally and still understand who you are. Your private life should be a reflection of who you are in your professional life and vice versa. Why? Because when your external reflects your internal and your internal reflects your external, that's where you find true success, happiness, satisfaction, and contentment.

When you achieve that level of authenticity and become wholly one person, the doors of the universe will open. The opportunities you're presented with, the people you meet, even the things you attract will be life altering—because the magnetism within your truthfulness and authenticity will pull the best of the best to you.

Authenticity also feeds off itself, helping you build authentic relationships—because you're no longer preoccupied with what you should do or how you're expected to behave in a particular situation or with a particular person. People trust you more because they know exactly who you are. There's no guesswork involved or peeling back the layers of "you" to get to the true you. When you're authentic, guesswork is unnecessary.

You're saying, *Here's who I am, and we don't need to agree on things or like each other—and that's okay. Let's just be authentic.* An approach like this makes life so much more manageable. But being authentic in this day and age isn't nearly as easy as it sounds.

Barriers to Authenticity

As I said, being authentic is one hell of an undertaking. Different forces, whether societal, cultural, familial, or religious, are constantly at work battling against you showing your true authentic self. You're expected to be a certain individual culturally, another one religiously, and another one professionally, organizationally, and societally.

But now it's time to shift that thinking. Veer away from those expectations, leave them behind, and be yourself. Which brings us to the most important question: Who are you?

It might sound like an innocuous query, but it's one that's actually pretty loaded. Or, in the words of too many social media relationship statuses to count, "It's complicated."

You may find that you don't know who the hell you are because you've been so bogged down being different people for different people. It's only natural, then, to number one, lose a sense of who you are; number two, forgo authenticity; and number three, lack satisfaction in life. For example, if religious Jane conflicts with organizational Jane, and societal Jane is constantly at odds with cultural Jane, how do you expect Jane to ever feel content?

You have to be comfortable in your skin and confident enough to claim who you are. It may not be to other people's liking or expectations, but that's okay. Be unapologetic about it. That doesn't make you rude, self-absorbed, or unempathetic.

It makes you someone who has self-respect and self-worth. It means you're someone who values yourself as a human and who deserves respect and has the right to live how you choose and be who you want to be. Because who you present yourself as is also a choice. You get to choose how you're going to behave at home, at work, in society, and economically. These are choices you make every single day, maybe without even realizing.

I'll be honest. Being authentic took a lot of courage for me—and getting to that point sucked nearly forty years of my life and required many brutally honest conversations. The religious Shuaib often conflicted with work Shuaib, or cultural Shuaib conflicted with societal Shuaib. Soon I began to dislike who I was. But for me, that was the biggest puzzle of all: *Who are you?* I kept asking myself. *Who the fuck are you, Shuaib Ahmed?*

Finding Your Authentic Self

Discovering who you truly are is just that—a discovery process. As I said, the true you is probably buried deep beneath layers of expectations established over decades from all facets of your life. In the process, your true self has likely become etched in the sedimentary rocks of the past.

So how do you find out who you truly are? Personally, I found that my childhood carried the most significant answers to my true self, because it was a time in my life, and I think most people's, where emotions aren't premeditated. They are instinctive and instant.

Looking back, I think about what things sparked emotions of happiness. What things made me fearful, what made me angry. What did I naturally gravitate toward? What excited me? What made me light up?

Those childhood emotions may give you a clue into your true self like they did for me.

Also try this exercise: close your eyes and imagine you're in a room by yourself. What would you say? How would you describe yourself? Who would you say you are?

During my divorce, I recall waking up in the middle of the night, looking into the mirror and asking myself, *Who the fuck are you? What do you stand for?* I hurriedly opened my notes app on my cell phone to answer these questions. I had nothing … I just left a blank note.

Then I tried an exercise that I encourage you to try as well. Either on your computer, tablet, or cell phone, or those big, white, blank, square things they call paper, make two columns. In the first, write *Who Am I*. In the second, write *Source*. For the Who Am I column, think of all the different words that define you and write them in this column. Then for each descriptor, in the Source column, write where those descriptions of you originated from. For example, you could write family, friends, culture, religion, self, etc. Once you're done, go back to the Source column and tally up how many of those descriptors originated from "self." I bet you'll be surprised by results. I sure as hell was.

At the risk of sounding cliche, the second way I'd encourage you to identify yourself is by listening to your heart. It has the answers you're seeking—you just have to be brave enough to hear and accept them.

No doubt there are a ton of people living my story, feeling inauthentic, but also remaining silent and feeling compelled to put on a performance and adhere to a cookie-cutter life. They live day-by-day exactly how they're told; outwardly they appear happy, but inwardly they feel turmoil, dissatisfaction, and frustration. They're living life on autopilot, going through the motions out of obligation and responsibility. To those people, I hear you. I know the struggle. I've lived it. This book was partly written for that very purpose, to help those individuals free themselves from those debilitating emotions!

It's time to have a critical dialogue and authentic conversation. And if you're not ready for that, you're not ready for the rest of this book. And that's okay. Put it away; come back when you're ready to have that talk. And if that time doesn't come immediately, maybe right now isn't the time in your life for you to be focusing on this conversation. That's fine too. But I assure you, at some point in your life, there's going to come a time where you'll arrive at a crossroads like I did and seek guidance. You might find yourself asking questions like, *Who am I? What am I doing here? What's my purpose?* That's when you'll know it's time to return to this book.

CHAPTER 3

The Birth of the ASA Way

AFTER LAW SCHOOL, I kicked off my career as a partner at a local law firm. With just me and no kids, life fell into an easy, manageable routine. That's how it typically is at that phase in life: a select few aspects demand your attention, and you're able to efficiently manage them. But after my kids were born, it felt like I'd been tossed in a money booth on a timer, trying to pocket whatever I could while the rest slipped through my grasp and whirled mockingly around me. Both halves of my life came head to head. On one hand, there was my career, which in its own right was like a brand-spanking-new child: young, just kicking off, and demanding boatloads of attention to grow and thrive. And then there was my actual flesh and blood: young humans I'd helped bring into the world and who needed and deserved my love, care, and attention. I felt like I'd been physically ripped in half, my mind constantly taunting me: *Which child will you give attention to today?*

Anyone with more than one kid knows it's impossible to evenly split time between them all, which is what I felt I was trying to do. It boiled down to my first option being me working long hours and pouring tremendous time into work, knowing that all said and done, my kids would have stronger chances, richer resources to draw from, and the head start in life I never did—but all at the risk of being an absent parent, forgoing quality time with them and missing out on significant milestones, which I could see them resenting me for later.

Here's the thing about kids: they don't remember what you buy them or the opportunities you create for them as a result of sacrifice—that appreciation comes much later in life, when they become parents themselves. The moments they'll most cherish and that will remain permanently etched in their brains is the quality time you invest with them. Which brought me to my other alternative: to pour more time into my kids, be present for the milestones, and be a father through and through … at the expense of punching out on the dot and subsequently being overlooked for promotions because my seniors perceived me to be a noncommittal, lackadaisical employee who doesn't give it his all, unlike John Doe in the corner office, who pitches fort in his cubicle and very likely brushes and bathes in the office restroom. I found myself experiencing the struggle of being a father while trying to still remain relevant and be viewed as a team player in an organization.

> I found myself experiencing the struggle of being a father while trying to still remain relevant and be viewed as a team player in an organization.

Suddenly I went from feeling completely in control of my future and career to being thrust into a tailspin. I was frustrated as a father and couldn't even begin to imagine how women and new moms endured making such an unfair decision between choosing their career—something they'd been groomed for and worked toward their entire adult life—and their child, an innocent party in it all.

I wanted to tackle both uncompromisingly: build something from the ground up for my kids but also somehow remain present in their lives. But I knew in expecting that, I was only fooling myself: in the current system, it was impossible to achieve both. When I was with my kids, my mind would wander to work, and on the nights I was putting in heavy hours to prove my commitment to my career, I couldn't stop my eyes from straying to the clock as I mentally tallied everything I was missing out on: soccer games, school plays, bedtime. No matter where I was, I felt torn and overridden with guilt. And no matter how I diced it up, I was always on the losing end.

Throughout the years, like most workers in corporate America, I'd experienced some toxic work cultures along the way. I'd never forgotten what that felt like—the destructive environment, the throwing your fellow employee under the bus to get ahead—and how it all ebbed into my personal life, affecting my disposition at home. I remember feeling unhappy, being engulfed by anxiety, and experiencing Sunday-night blues, which let me tell you is a real-as-fuck phenomenon. However, I made it through because of a mentor who was also the managing partner. He was inspirational, a great leader, and someone whom I could talk to for hours on end discussing how to be a better attorney as well as various facets of life and business. Despite that, I could not endure the incompatible culture at the firm.

Finally, one day I saw an opportunity to break free. No longer did I have to work for someone else. I could be my own boss.

When I made up my mind to start my own practice, I made a concerted effort to keep those emotions raw and fresh in my mind—and I made a promise to myself that no one in my organization would ever feel the way I had so long as I was navigating the ship. Honestly, I found that to be less difficult than I anticipated. And with my naani's teachings as my bedrock, engrained deep within every part and fiber of me, it was more than achievable. The ASA Way, as I would later call it, was already a part of me, deep rooted in my mind long before the thought of starting a practice stemmed into reality. For instance, empathy was never a problem, coming naturally in nearly every situation, no matter where I was—at the grocery store parking lot, helping an elderly woman locate her car or at work, listening to a coworker commiserate about her dog's deteriorating health.

That combined with my relentless thirst for knowledge and improvement set me on a path to improving not only my life but the lives of those around me. I fed my hunger to improve by devouring books on growth and how to be a good human. Slowly I realized that each of these reinforced the teachings of my naani, a woman who'd never once crossed paths with the business world, let alone understood the first thing about it. Yet she'd somehow known it all.

With that dawning realization came the understanding that these inherent teachings, which had morphed into traits, had always and would always be my pathway and guiding light to everything I did in life. They were a part of me organically, deep rooted before any research existed on the benefits of these behaviors. Regardless of where I was—work, home, gym, or elsewhere—they would forever remain a part of me.

I believe everything in your life has a purpose that exists to prepare you for something bigger. In hindsight, I'm convinced those early years with my naani were a launchpad, preparing, honing, and molding me to one day become a leader. Now that the opportunity was within reach, I wanted to put my position to use and make it so no one at my firm ever felt compelled to choose one part of their life over the other.

I set to work putting these ideologies into play with my very first employee, who is now our director of operations. At the time I was barely able to afford her salary. As we added staff, keeping that message alive became a challenge I wanted to solve, and quickly. With just one employee, I was dealing with just one personality, which isn't all too difficult. Besides, she was wired like me in that we both worked to the bone to make sure the business succeeded. It didn't matter what time of day or day of the week, business came first. Managing her was very easy. But scaling to five, ten, twenty or more employees meant dealing with a whole slew of idiosyncrasies, changing the dynamics. But I was dogged in maintaining my original mindset, which could not and would not ever change. All I had to do now was figure out how to root it within the organization. No matter how big we got or how many people we added, I never wanted to lose sight of the central theme of what made us great: that we truly cared about one another as individuals. And that we are all created equal no matter how unique the challenges and struggles we faced or no matter how different our titles or positions within the firm, which shouldn't ever be a factor in any of it.

I wanted to develop a process that not only encouraged employees to live both parts of their lives to the fullest, personal and professional—but also find a way to nourish each one.

And that's how the ASA Way was born.

Applying a Holistic Approach

When we talk about the ASA Way, we're talking about conjoining both the personal and professional parts of our lives. The aim is to join them in a cohesive, complementary way, maximizing success in both and empowering you to be the best version of yourself at all times as an employee, employer, husband/wife, father/mother, and in every other integral role you play. But the only way that's even possible is because the ASA Way adopts a holistic approach. Let me give you an example.

If you were to consult a medical professional or approach anyone off the street and ask them to define holistic medicine, nine times of out ten, people will probably be able to tell you what it is or give you a good gist about what it means. They might tell you it's different parts of your life that have to be healthy, not just physiologically, but mentally and emotionally too. Holistic medicine isn't about popping pills like they're Tic Tacs. It's about examining all parts of your life and ensuring each is calibrated with the other so you can reap the best results from a medical perspective.

Now let me toss you a curveball and ask this: What's holistic law? What's holistic corporate America? Ask those questions of anyone, and they'll think you've lost your mind. Because that's how far removed our thinking is. There's no such thing as holistic corporate America or law—those words don't even seem to jibe well together in the same sentence.

But imagine if your doctor diagnosed you with depression and prescribed you a pill. Then every time you came in for a follow-up visit, all they did was ask you questions like, *Did you take the pill? What time did you take it? Where were you when you took it?* And that was the gist of the examination. They never delved beneath the surface to uncover your lifestyle, relationships, sleep habits, triggers—would you ever get a sense that they actually cared about you as a person, apart from achieving the desired prognosis for their reports?

Obviously, the medical profession is a multibillion-dollar industry that's somehow able to create a platform where people feel accepted enough to confide in their doctors about the most personal aspects of their lives.

Get the perspective of a well-reputed doctor, like my brothers, and they'll tell you these questions empower them to devise an effective treatment plan that complements every part of a patient's life. In fact, one of my brothers, who is a physician, spends an hour or more on each initial consultation! More power to you, bro! Now take the same reasoning and apply it to the way we're running corporations, businesses, and the legal industry—we're certainly not delving deep. In fact we're working the other way around. We're treating employees like robots, setting expectations that, when they aren't met, have repercussions on bonuses or annual increases or promotions. We're not delving beyond day-to-day job responsibilities to get to the root of each person, who they are, what moves and motivates them, what makes them sad, happy, angry, euphoric. We're basically asking them to stuff a sock in it and do their job— no complaints. We don't care about hobbies or personal problems. We care only about promoting a transactional, superficial, and unempathetic relationship.

That approach needs to be buried six feet under with good ol' pagers and rotary phones. It's old fashioned and doesn't work, and it sure as hell

> **The hard truth is this: there's no holistic approach to corporate America—and that's what the ASA Way is here to change.**

doesn't retain employees or keep them happy. So you can toss out any prospect of those disgruntled, frustrated employees making your clients happy in the long run. Keep to this approach, and I can guarantee you big-time turnover and money wasted on an endless cycle of rehiring and retraining employees, which will create a hell of a mess for your bottom line. The hard truth is this: there's no holistic approach to corporate America—and that's what the ASA Way is here to change.

The ASA Way = The Holistic Way

The ASA Way accounts for everything we talk about when we look at someone in a holistic fashion, seeing them for all the composite parts and pieces that come together to make them who they are. This includes everything from the food they eat to what time they go to bed—because all of that is interrelated and determines an individual, their well-being, and their peace of mind.

The premise of the ASA Way is that every aspect of life is interconnected. There's no such thing as aligning the personal here and the professional there. If you think about it, there's no such thing as a line of separation in the medical practice when it comes to sifting through those parts of your life. No one warns doctors that they shouldn't ask how many pets you have because it has nothing to do with medicine. Being able to mimic that approach in corporate America, whether in the legal industry or in general, will deliver better results long term.

This is where you're probably wondering about the damage to your pocketbook to implement a program like this. But the cost is minimal, if anything. I was able to adopt this approach from day one as a solo practitioner with barely enough to kickstart a law practice. Today we're a team of twenty. Although this approach is ideal for businesses of any size from small to large and the financial investment is infinitesimal, it does require resources by way of emotional intelligence, time, and effort in getting to know your staff. Most of all, it requires you to care.

So if you're still hell bent on nothing except how this affects your bottom line, with complete disregard for any of the things I've mentioned, the ASA Way probably isn't for you. If that's the case, I'm willing to bet my last dollar that five years from now, you won't be in business. That might sound harsh, but I'd rather give it to you straight and hope I'm successful in jolting you awake to what's to come than have you fall flat because no one was truthful or bold enough to warn you. Because perhaps before, obliviousness and disregard were somewhat acceptable. But now, post-COVID-19, they inarguably, absolutely, and without a doubt are not. In the time it took for the world to quarantine and reemerge into a new landscape, several businesses shifted how they accommodate, care for, and show compassion toward employees, the uproar around social justice serving as a prime example.

Never before has corporate America rallied behind a cause as fervently as they have of late. But why the sudden interest? Sure, they care, but I'd argue they also realize the importance of not only how their voice impacts society in general but also how the message they're sending is interpreted by their employees. Employees, no doubt, are thrilled to be part of an organization that champions a just cause; it boosts morale and makes them feel they're part of something bigger and more dynamic than just an object that helps boost the company's bottom line.

My argument is this: Why not expand those efforts to every single individual who works so hard day in, day out for your company without needing a big event to champion behind to show you care? Being empathetic and caring should be an inbred part of any company—that's the right way to do business moving forward. But for whatever reason, we still find ourselves stuck in a rut, guards up, feeling like we have no business knowing about people's personal affairs, when those very affairs affect so much about your employee and their performance as well as their contentment as a human. Conversely, employees feel like employers have no business knowing their personal matters, because there's a huge line of mistrust there.

The ASA Way talks through these hurdles and empowers you to not only address employees' personal lives but also their professional lives. And if you're an employee, this approach helps your employer acknowledge and understand that you have a life and existence as an individual and that you come with unique struggles, obligations, and responsibilities.

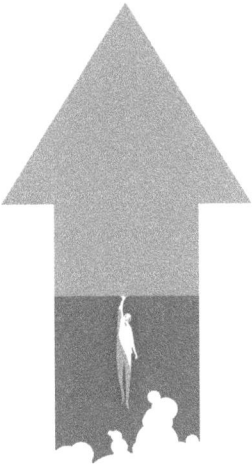

PART II:
The ASA Way Process

CHAPTER 4

Know What Matters; Hold It Close

My first understanding of culture came from my grandmother. She cultivated it in our home, but not in the sense of customs and rituals. The culture she created gave a specific feeling and ambiance to our home. One of warmth, safety, and no judgments, where people, me included, could talk about anything they felt like and express however they felt without shame or embarrassment. You could feel this energy as soon as you walked through the door.

Naani never chided or ridiculed me anytime I cried. Instead she encouraged these expressions of emotion, telling me it was okay to be angry or sad, as long as we followed it up with communication. As a result of this culture, I've never forgotten the feeling of that home.

It wasn't until I moved to my home in the US that I realized just how much culture could influence or impede progress and development. In the culture my grandmother fostered, I'd flourished. When I moved from there into a culture with opposite attitudes and beliefs, I struggled.

When I launched my organization, the first thing that sprung to my mind as I skimmed the unfurnished square footage of office space, the sound of my steps echoing off the walls, was my naani's home. Here I was about to start something from the ground up that, God willing, would employ and help many people. I could directly impact people's professional and personal lives. How did I want them to feel the moment they walked through those doors? What attitudes and beliefs did I want to shape my organization? What could I instill that would help everyone spending the majority of their day here to flourish?

Even before we'd opened for business, I was thinking about the one thing that would shape my entire organization's persona: culture.

Defining Culture

When we talk about culture, people perceive it to be an almost unspoken, natural way about a company or organization. But culture is an intentional, purposeful thing. It's what makes people stay when the going gets tough. Because in the end, money is never enough. Sure, initially it's what might attract your employees to the job, but it's ultimately how they feel when they're there with you, by your side, that their minds absorb, shaping their attitudes and impressions about your organization and how empowered, productive, and happy it makes them feel.

Ask yourself, *How can I create a healthy work culture? What does that look like? What can my organization do to enforce that culture on a daily basis?*

For me, promoting cross collaboration was important, which is why I opted for an open-concept floor plan. To go along with that, I implemented a writing-on-the-wall concept, a space where employees could literally write on the wall to promote idea sharing and garner feedback from others versus writing thoughts on sheets of paper that can't be so easily shared or seen. But I'm getting ahead of myself.

First, let's talk about how I even came to determine this culture for my organization. How exactly do you build a company culture? Where do you even start? I have a simple, effective way to kick us off.

A Story of Values

My naani was a woman of values. She was uncompromising to a fault in ensuring her every action and decision aligned perfectly with those values, which she clung to unyieldingly. Most of those values were rooted in religion, others were culturally driven, and a few were personal choices. When I think back to Naani's values, I remember in particular taking a stroll every morning down the bumpy, uneven streets of India, clogged with pedestrians, rickshaws, cars, and buses polluting smoke in our faces as we went on our way buying fresh produce from the local "market."

This wasn't your neighborhood Whole Foods or Sprouts. In India, *market* was a term loosely used to refer to a collection of produce carts huddled together in a designated area. These trips both drove me apeshit mad and, at the same time, humbled me to no end—because they were the perfect example of Naani's endless reservoir of patience and goodness.

It's a known fact that everything in these markets is always negotiable. Want to buy produce? Negotiable. Want to buy jewelry? Negotiable. Want to buy the shirt off someone's back? That, too, was negotiable! You get the picture. Bargaining is not only expected, it's anticipated—a part of the cultural norm. So if a vendor quoted you a hundred rupees ($1.37 in American dollars) for five pounds of tomatoes, you could bet your life he'd jacked up the price a few notches, expecting you to negotiate him down. All around us, people would be haggling to no end for everything from watermelon to green beans. They'd walk away, in most cases, with a good deal at a fraction of the original quoted price. That was the case for almost everyone, that is, except my naani. Although we barely had enough most days, and every penny mattered, she refused to bargain. Every day, the person ahead of us would walk away paying a third the amount we did for double the quantity.

And here would come Naani, forking over from her beaten wallet every last paisa of whatever they asked without a word of protest.

When the vendors caught on that she'd pay whatever they requested, she quickly became their favorite. It seemed whatever losses they'd tallied from the previous handful of customers, they'd aim to make up for from her. The moment they saw her, they hiked the prices, which seemed excessive and ridiculous sometimes. And still she never uttered a word.

Every day I'd walk to that market clinging to her hand, and every day I would return home seething. "How come you never bargain with them, Naani?" I'd protest. "How come everyone else gets to pay so much less for the same thing? We're not made of money, just like the others. But they negotiate—how come you don't?"

Her reply was always the same. "Maybe they have needs that surpass ours, so they have no choice but to negotiate," she'd reply.

CHAPTER 4: KNOW WHAT MATTERS; HOLD IT CLOSE

"We don't have much either," I'd argue.

"True. But if I haggled, I would be stealing some of their livelihood to protect my own," she'd say. "How could I do that?"

The beauty of it was that despite always coming out on the losing end of the pricing game, Naani was never remorseful against the person who paid less than she did nor the vendors who screwed us out of a few extra rupees every day. It wasn't until much later that I realized she wasn't losing: she was winning by handfuls at the game of life. Her willingness to tolerate her situation so easily was because these actions were in line with her value system.

Looking back, I also recall more trying times where her commitment to her values remained unwavering. Like the evenings my naana was in one of his many dark moods. His voice would bellow out from their room, loud, angry, berating. I was pretty certain all the neighbors surrounding us could hear his shrieking loud and clear as he screamed about the inanest things. Sometimes what he said would baffle me, because his accusations were unfair and often baseless, having no rhyme or reason to hold anyone, let alone Naani, accountable for.

There were times I was tempted to bust open the door, punch him in the gut as hard as I could, and set him straight. It took everything in me to restrain myself. But never once did Naani utter a peep. She let him rant and rave, listening quietly. When he was through, she'd come out of the room, shoulders hunched, a look of complete defeat on her face and an ocean of tears brimming in her eyes. But she never spoke up for herself or argued back. Empathy and patience were part of her value systems, even at the expense of her own happiness. Any time I questioned why she never stood up to him, especially when we all knew he was dead in the wrong for lashing out at her most of the time, she'd shake her head. "Maybe there's something he's going through that's worse than any of us can understand or imagine," she'd say. "Maybe this is his way of venting out his frustrations." Her values, no matter how much I begged to disagree with them at times, were uncompromising. It was part frustrating, part awe inspiring to see how beautifully she stayed loyal to them.

You might be thinking, *Hey, wait. We're in the middle of talking about the ASA Way. What does any of this have to do with this ground-breaking process that's going to empower me to transform myself and/or my business?*

Good question. And the answer is that the entire backbone of the ASA Way is about values—they're what hold it up. And values are what will and should help shape your company's culture. Many of the things we do in our lives, from the decisions we make to how we approach situations, depend on our values—irrespective of whether you're an employee or an employer. Values are, or should be, the underpinnings of every individual and, yes, every organization. They are your guiding light, your compass, your template, laying the groundwork and pointing you to the direction that's right for you based on what matters to you.

> **Values are, or should be, the underpinnings of every individual and, yes, every organization.**

Metaphorically speaking, values are the first layer of the ASA Way process. Establishing values is like pouring the foundation for everything that's to come in the following chapters—it'll keep the rest erect, stable, and strong. Without the foundation, the rest collapses. So if you're tempted to skip this chapter and move ahead, do me a favor. Don't skip this chapter and move ahead. Otherwise you'll be erecting some incredible, quality framework on unstable ground.

Having a Real-as-Fuck Conversation with Yourself about Values

Post-divorce, one of the first questions I asked myself was, *What are my values? What is my firm's value system?*

It didn't escape me that, though I was inching toward forty, it was the first time I'd ever given the question any thought. I'd never had an honest conversation with myself—a conversation every employee and individual needs to have with themselves—about what my value system or principles were. Until then I'd been living life with my head stuck in a box, allowing people to guide me based on *their* principles and beliefs. I never gambled because it went against my parents' beliefs. I didn't drink because my wife didn't like it. I'd never looked past these prohibitions to once question which principles resonated with me and which ones I was blindly accepting just because.

That day, for the first time ever, I put pen to paper and defined my values. These were not religious values or cultural values. These were Shuaib's values. Just the ring of that felt liberating. I felt like I was flying free, untethered to influence, and completely empowered to design my life based on the things that mattered most to me.

Right then I had a shameless, uncompromising, and completely sincere conversation with myself. I knew there were certain things I'd never done because religiously they were shunned. Certain things I didn't do because culturally they were taboo. But now that I was free from those shackles, what would I define as my own value systems?

If you're someone who's never practiced this exercise before, you should.

Without values, you have no direction and no way of identifying what you stand for—in essence, you stand for nothing, which can cause indecisiveness and poor decision-making, since there's nothing to guide you.

From an individual standpoint, that wasn't acceptable to me any longer. And from an organizational standpoint, no way in hell was that okay by me. I wanted a value system and one that I could lean on and incorporate throughout every fiber of my organization. I wanted every decision, everything we did from the smallest to the largest actions, to be guided through that lens. Based on what mattered to me and what I gave the most fucks about, I came up with a value system.

How to Come Up with a Value System

It really doesn't matter whether you're an employee or employer—values serve the same purpose for everyone: they drive action. Say, for example, you're job hunting. Having a defined value system will propel you toward organizations that share your principles.

I'll be the first to admit that when I initially kicked off, I established the value system for our firm, but as we scaled, I wasn't the sole party responsible for expanding upon those initial values. My employees had a great hand in the value system we have in place today. You might be thinking, *Wait, you trusted your employees, the people who literally have a fraction of the skin in your company that you do, to help you pen its value system?* The answer is a resounding yes. And I felt comfortable enough giving them that power because, as I said, I knew from the get-go that every employee I'd hired already shared the values I did, so I had absolutely no qualms or apprehension about entrusting them to the task. Further, the only real way to assure that your employees will adhere to your company's values is if those values are also shared by them. Otherwise it is nothing more than a formality.

Honestly, your value system can't and shouldn't be something your organization drums up single handedly. Sure, as a leader or owner, your take on your organization's values should matter. But if they don't resonate with your employees, you should be open to reassessing them—because not only will those values drive the organization's actions, but they'll also drive the decisions and actions of your employees. And if your employees aren't sold on those values wholeheartedly, they'll deliver on them only half-heartedly, if at all.

The same goes for you.

Every resource, every decision, almost everything you do should somehow link to one of your core values—because without those guiding principles, you'll be jumping around like a bunny on Easter, hopping toward one direction one moment and another the next.

I've seen organizations do this. They start with one idea then scratch it and venture in a totally different direction. I get it. You're always going to make improvements in your process; evolution and growth is the name of the game. But you can't scrap things midway and jump the bandwagon on something else because that creates *inconsistency*. And inconsistency is just as detrimental to your organization, employees, and customers as consistency is beneficial. "What's going on with that business?" they'll say. "We're hearing different things; we're seeing different things; we're not even sure we understand this organization or what it stands for." A value system you stick to like jam to bread will ameliorate the risk of this type of mixed messaging.

As an employee, it works the same: values are integral. You have to know your value system like you know the size of your underwear, because otherwise you risk bouncing around from job to job, waiting for the perfect one. What you need to realize right now is that the perfect job will only materialize when your values align with an organization's. It's like getting married. You don't marry someone you don't understand just because they look good. We all know how that ends. You go for a person because you connect with them, you feel understood, and you understand them. You feel one with them. And yeah, if they've got a hot body or nice hair, no harm, no foul. In the same way, compensation cannot be the sole determining criteria of where you want to go in your career. Ask yourself, *Which organization do I want to work for? Do I align with this organization? Does the organization align with me? Do we have that balance?*

Whether you're an employer or employee, know your values; hold them close. They have to be so near and dear to you that it becomes almost effortless to make a decision using them as your guiding principles. Ultimately they should serve as your framework within which to evaluate every decision you make—and that's what shapes your culture.

Put Your Money Where Your Values Are

If you go job hunting now or in the future, I'll offer you a piece of advice: do not just eye the compensation package and say, yeah, that seems like a decent chunk of change. I accept.

As I said, nothing will ever be enough in terms of financial gain—that's just human nature. And hell yeah, compensation is important, but what will give you a greater sense of peace of mind, belonging, and purpose is working for an organization whose value system aligns with yours—one you feel you can respect and feel connected with. That should be your focus when you're interviewing potential employers. Because if not, the buzz of a hefty paycheck will eventually wear off, and you'll be left miserable in an organization where you feel like a misfit in the long run.

The same is true if you're an organization—break beyond the boundaries of conventional interviewing. When I interview potential employees, I rarely glance at their résumés. Because honestly, there isn't a damned person out there whose résumé doesn't make them sound like they're deserving of the Nobel Prize. Every last candidate I've ever seen looks amazing on paper, but that doesn't tell me much about who they are. Neither do references, because the chances you'll put a reference on your application who's going to tell me that you're a sucky-ass person or employee are probably slim to none.

Compensation is important, but what will give you a greater sense of peace of mind, belonging, and purpose is working for an organization whose value system aligns with yours.

What I do instead is focus on letting candidates do the talking so I can get a glimpse into their value systems and what's most meaningful to them. What do they stand for? What drives them? What inspires them? What system or principles are the bedrock of their beliefs and lead them when they're against a critical decision? Ultimately what I'm trying to determine is whether the values of our firm align with the candidate's.

Here's the kicker: many people believe they have certain attitudes and beliefs, and they may "ace" the interview in convincing you of that. But in practice, perhaps they're not exactly as they believe. What do you do in that case? My advice is to do what you would if an employee weren't performing as they should: take the loss and part ways. Sure, it'll be a loss on paper, and you'll be down one person in productivity, and they may be a supertalented individual, but to protect the culture you've worked so hard to create for your organization, you have to be bold enough to take that step and be uncompromising.

But why take an approach that deviates completely from tried and tested interview practices? What does it achieve? Let's talk about that.

Letting Values Be Your Guiding Light

When onboarding an employee, one of the first things companies do is flood them with trainings to articulate the company's values and how to live them daily, all while praying that at the end of the day, the employee buys into them and makes them their own. With the ASA Way approach, I can toss that entire "training" piece out the window—because we know their values are our values even before they walk through our doors. There's no buying or selling into anything.

Number two, whatever decisions are made by the organization make organic sense to the team when everyone shares the same guiding principles. This shared similarity gives employees a better sense of how the organization thinks, which lenses it views decisions through, and in which direction its thought processes naturally gravitate.

Making decisions through defined values also leads to a level of consistency in how and what you, as leadership, deliver—which is huge. Because consistency breeds trust, which is essential in the leader-employee relationship.

That consistency travels beyond your employees to customers and third parties. They see the same messages and patterns, which they come to then expect from you. They gain a sense of how your firm operates.

But sometimes sticking to your values, no matter how well defined, can be tougher than we think, so it's important to take a step back every now and again to see how you're faring.

Every October, the team and I head off for a retreat to … wait for it … Wisconsin. I know it's not the most glamorous place, but it's a sneeze away from Chicago, and it serves the purpose of a place where we can all sit back, let loose, and reassess our values and how we've made decisions within them. Or if we've somehow fallen outside the boundaries of them, we pause to see how we can step back in and seal those boundaries tighter or readjust them so we don't tumble outside of them again.

Let me make this clear: this is not a time where I lecture employees about what we should do better. It's an opportunity for employees to tell me and each other what we can do better. We jot down the ideas and then identify the ones we want to tackle the following year. This process fosters a culture of inclusivity—employees know their voices matter, are heard, and make a difference in the direction the organization will venture.

How to Build Culture through Values

Once we started the ASA Way and identified our values as the first step, the next step was to brainstorm how we could incorporate those values in our organization to make them a part of our culture. Values are a set of principles or beliefs that are important to you. Culture is putting those values into play through tangible actions that can be seen and felt.

For instance, one of our values was promoting a mixture of work and life into one's lifestyle. Notice I didn't say work-life balance. Why? Because work-life balance is the biggest piece of bullshit ever. There's no precise formula to devote exactly the same amount of time to both parts of your life. Many organizations spew the lingo, but the demands they toss at you seem completely at odds with this term, with work sucking up the majority of your time. Many of these same companies have employees logging in evenings and weekends, when family time should be the only priority. At a time when many workers are working from home due to the pandemic, this "balance" has been knocked down on its head, with employees working more than ever! At my firm, I won't stand for any of it. I wanted to cultivate an environment where empowered employees could embrace the most from both worlds.

Even though there's no way to 100 percent balance both, I knew I could at least leverage that value to somehow create a culture that alleviated the stress of employees feeling compelled to work the long, hard hours attorneys are notoriously known to. To achieve that, I tackled the main culprit: billable hours. The industry norm is for attorneys to bill anywhere from 2,100 to 2,800 hours a year. That's a lot of fucking hours. At ASA, I knew it would be counterintuitive to desire a good work-life mix (because, come on, that's just a better term) and still have an absurd requirement like that. Because I held true to that value, I lowered our billing requirements. How? Simple. Reduce overhead, get rid of the fat, get lean. No one cares about your fancy office overlooking the lake and expensive, robot-looking coffee machines! Clients want exceptional service at a reasonable cost. That's it. We now have one of the lowest billing requirements in the industry. This means lower caseloads for attorneys and more time for family. Sure, I'm giving up revenue in the short term. But in the long term, I'm gaining a kick-ass, productive team with top-notch talent constantly elbowing to get in through our doors.

And if you look around, you'll notice the employees we currently have are sticking around longer; they're not burning out or wallowing in misery, and they're not a pain in the ass to be around. The next time you pass by your local courthouse, I dare you to find a single lawyer who fits this description. My point: having a relentless commitment to your values makes a difference, even if in the short run you end up losing a bit of money.

Gratitude is another value of ours. To make it part of our culture, we tied an action to it: creating a gratitude box. Of course, after COVID-19, when work became virtual, so did our gratitude box. Now it's less of a box and more of a channel that's accessible on mobile devices. Every day, I see a stream of messages filter in on this channel, which is the greatest feeling. Basically, the gratitude box/channel is a place where staff and attorneys can post thank-you notes for teammates. I could thank my assistant for staying late and getting an item knocked off my to-do list. Or a coworker could thank someone for helping them out with a case. Pre-COVID-19, when we hosted monthly huddles, we'd select a restaurant or someplace fun to unleash the contents of the box. We'd go around the table and have each person pick out a note at random and read it aloud.

Yeah, the gratitude box aligns with our value of gratitude, but it also achieves a couple of other things. First, it's rewarding to hear someone say, "Thank you." Many of the tasks we do day to day are pretty mundane, sometimes tedious, and often thankless. So a heartfelt thank-you goes a long way. Second, it makes the person you're writing the note to appreciate you, building camaraderie between colleagues. It's one thing to verbally thank someone and another entirely to go out of your way to write a note. Third, it draws attention for us as an organization to all the incredible ways our staff is going above and beyond on a daily basis. Efforts that would otherwise go unseen, unnoticed, and unaccredited. To be able to pause and acknowledge and show appreciation to staff who are going above the call of duty is something we never want to lose as an organization. Fourth, and most important, it forces you to think that you don't have it so fucking bad! It is easy to look at an organization and point to numerous things that can be better … better pay, better benefits, less work, etc. Gratitude instantly humbles you and makes you realize just how damn blessed you really are!

You must be uncompromising with your values, even at times when it seems the most challenging. For instance, the year after the initial COVID-19 outbreak, I was analyzing the firm's quarter-one financials. As a team, we did not meet our goals. In fact we were falling severely short revenue-wise. How did we respond? Did we fire attorneys who failed to meet the friendly billable requirement? Did we place employees on furlough to account for the lack of receivables? Nope. Instead I personally sat down with each employee to discuss their thoughts on our quarter-one team performance and dissected some of the challenges they were facing at work and home. After those meaningful conversations, it was obvious that people were experiencing some serious burnout dealing with work and home. Examining our values of promoting wellness and holistic health, I decided I needed to take action to ensure we were tying them to our culture.

We got to work, reaching out to clients to tell them we'd be available via email but that our office would be closed on a specific date. Then we surprised our staff with complimentary massages at the local spa so they could kick back and unwind. To make sure they didn't fret about losing out on pay for the day, we gave them credit for their billing. By doing this, I was reinforcing the message that our value of promoting holistic health was real. That it was so real, we were willing to forgo a day of revenue during a poor fiscal quarter to ensure our employees had a day to decompress. In return, our employees sensed our care and concern for them as people. Having a law firm do this today may be unheard of, but to me nothing makes greater sense. Caring for our employees in this way is our culture.

Stop Counting Pennies

I thought I'd pause right there and speak to you folks who have a hard time looking past your balance sheet. Because you're out there; I know you are. Yes, I get you're in the business of making money and maximizing revenue. So when I talk about short-term losses, I see you clutching your chest. Let me tell you this from experience: sacrificing short-term revenue, if it means being able to sustain not only your organization but also your people for the long haul, is more than worth it. I don't want my employees crying a puddle in the office, running to the ER in the middle of work because they think they're having a heart attack that ends up being an anxiety attack, or barreling out the door the first chance they get when my competitors come whistling. Even worse, I don't want them exiting the industry altogether after spending their entire college careers pumping money into student debt so they could one day call themselves an attorney.

I should also acknowledge that I understand that most organizations start with financials when contemplating a decision. Is this profitable? Is this lucrative? Will it make us look spectacular on paper? But with the ASA Way, financials are not the first part of the decision-making process. When we're making critical decisions at our firm, values are our starting point. Because if it doesn't fit there, then we're only lying to ourselves and our clients about who we are and what we're all about. We weigh every decision or action against our values, asking, *Does this fit within our value system?* If yes, then we proceed further in the process, which includes financials.

Other firms may argue that they don't want to shut down the office and lose out on revenue just so employees can indulge in a spa day, of all things. For me, I understand short term we'll be down a couple of figures—and that's okay. I'd rather have my employees feeling energized and empowered, knowing they're being taken care of, and subsequently feed that energy back into their families and work. That one day of revenue lost will return tenfold, because you'll have more productive, dedicated, happier employees who are loyal to you and to the success of your organization. How do I know? Because this approach has helped us triple our revenues in the long term from a boost in employee morale and productivity. And our organization and its success has become personal to our employees. We're no longer just any organization. We're the organization that sent care packages and offered extra time off when a loved one passed. The one that encouraged taking time when the children and homelife grew overwhelming. The one with its hand outstretched to help them fulfill their ambitions. Employees who are taken care of this way are going to think a thousand times before they walk out the door. Because you're no longer just an organization—you're their organization, and one they start to hold pride in.

One time, I was traveling and had a jam-packed calendar with tasks that needed to be completed against a deadline. When I finally got around to tackling them, I learned that someone else had already taken care of them—without me even having to request help.

If you're still iffy and fretting over profit margins, I can understand that's a tough mind space to come out of. I'll go as far as to acknowledge that yes, all of that is important, but with such a narrow approach to business, you'll miss out on the real messaging that will make all the difference for your company—in employee behaviors and subsequently in your bottom line. Because let's face it—your employees drive your bottom line. Period.

The other part of it is personal satisfaction. With a focus on value-driven decisions and the subsequent positive impact that has on your employees, there's no beating the feeling of utter satisfaction in knowing you're making a difference in the lives of your employees. You're not just increasing your profit margin. You're changing a life that affects so many other lives: families, children, spouses.

Your values should amplify your margins, not hinder them.

The other question that might be hammering through your mind is when value is first in your decision-making process, does that ever negatively affect your bottom line in the long run? That's a good question. And my answer to it is this: your values should amplify your margins, not hinder them. If you're not getting sustainable margins and revenue through the door, you may need to reevaluate your values. They should work in conjunction with your goals to boost your bottom line. But, and this is something that needs to be said loud and clear, you have to understand that sometimes values can be spot on—sticking to them may yield you results in, say, ninety days instead of the thirty you're hoping for. Be patient. Don't be shortsighted. If you're all about *now, now, now, now* and not at all focused on the long-term return versus maximizing short-term profits, you should probably take some business classes, because you probably won't be in business ten years from now. It's a truth I'd rather you swallow now and do something about rather than wait until it's too late.

I've been part of cutthroat organizations that were all about the bottom line—and it was terrible. They make you feel disposable, disrespected, almost worthless. I bet those organizations are the ones that sneak behind metallic doors, rev up their laptops, and identify employees by ID number in conversation. Because each person is nothing more than that to them: a number that inches them closer to their bottom line. Something is fundamentally wrong and totally fucked up with that approach. Unfortunately, it's an approach many organizations still adopt.

But, Shuaib, you might say. It's so much easier to talk the talk than walk the walk. I'll respond to that with a cliche of my own: you're preaching to the choir.

COVID-19 was one of the most trying times for us as a firm. I held a meeting at both my offices when it was clear that things were about to go south. "We're going to find a way to keep everybody on payroll," I promised my staff. "We're not laying off anyone, even if it means I don't take home a penny." Keep in mind that at this point, we were only about five years into the business, so it was still brand spanking new, with a ton of overhead weighing heavy on us.

And as we began slightly emerging from the pandemic, we were still trying to stay true to our holistic values and our financials, which seemed impossible to achieve at the time. Basically this meant that both during and even post-shutdown, we weren't shoving our doors wide open just yet. We wanted to be empathetic to people's personal situations, be cognizant that they had kids at home and elderly to care for, family members who'd passed away and whom they were still grieving. Going to them expecting the same level of revenue production because I wanted to boost my bottom line was simply not something I was willing to do or felt comfortable doing. And so I kept quiet. This presented a clear conflict, of course: it was either caring for the well-being of my employees or keeping the organization afloat.

The financials weren't pretty, as I mentioned previously. In fact, they were probably some of the worst statements I've had the displeasure of laying eyes on since I started the firm—I'd never seen so much red my entire life.

In the meantime, we were sending out weekly messages to check in on employees. Immediately they expressed appreciation for our concern regarding their health and mental wellness. Had I been a jerk and pressed them to work normal hours, pestered them for not meeting numbers, or disregarded their mental headspace, they'd likely be counting the days before they could apply for another job and get the hell out of there. I didn't want that.

Although the employees were as happy as they could be under the circumstances, our revenue was still declining. Finally, after putting it off as long as I could, I knew it was time to have a difficult conversation. I rounded up with the group and pulled up our revenues to present to them. "We can go about six more months before we'll be forced to pull the plug," I told them. That was the beginning and the end of our meeting. I left feeling defeated, scared shitless, and exhausted. But then, in the six months that followed, something remarkably strange happened. Not only did we make up the red, but we made a decent profit, considering a pandemic was still ravaging the world. Even better, every single employee received their year-end bonus and salary increases!

My point: because the organization had stepped in to take care of employees when they needed it most, they stepped in to take care of it when it needed it most. They couldn't stand to watch it or each other go down without a fight, so they rallied together and turned those numbers around without any prodding.

Did I sacrifice short term by opting to keep employees safe and not pressurized to work? Yes. But in the long run, I gained a tremendous amount in organization morale and profits—all because we stuck to our values, which fostered a powerful culture.

When you're having conversations with employees beyond just work about the deeper intricacies that wire them to be who they are, such as well-being, peace of mind, goals, family life, etc., you'll foster a remarkable culture unlike anything you can imagine.

The Better Tomorrow Is Not Coming; It's All on You

I'M GOING TO BE CANDID HERE—this chapter has some brutal truths. The quicker you accept them, the closer you inch toward embracing the ASA Way. But first, some context.

I haven't met a stronger human being than my naani. No matter how little we had, she never made excuses or blamed anyone for her situation. Not her husband or son for our limited resources, not the environment or society for the polluted water she had to boil daily to kill contamination, and never God for her circumstances or struggles.

She seized each day with discipline, never letting the things around her deter her day or her life. Then there was my uncle, a work demon and the epitome of a go-getter. He'd started a small travel agency out of nothing, making barely enough to put food on the table, but with the same discipline so characteristic of Naani, he was relentless. He worked nonstop, pushing his business until it flourished beyond what he or any of us could have imagined. His success transformed our living conditions and our lives. We went from living in a rundown five-hundred-square-foot flat to purchasing a beautiful place with a balcony overlooking the city. Also, my parents, who were first-generation East Indian immigrants, barely had enough when they came to the US and built successful businesses, including a medical practice and real estate investments.

All of them combined proved that anything was possible in life, and much of it is within our control. I grew up like this, surrounded by people who grabbed life by the wheels, never chancing their fate to the hands of others.

I remember my naani often asking me, *Where do you think money comes from, Shuaib? A tree?*

At the time, I was too young to process what she was saying … why would money grow on a tree? What brainiac came up with that? It was at the tip of my tongue to answer yes and ask her why we couldn't just plant a crop of them in our backyard. But something in the way she said it made me realize that wasn't the right answer.

That was Naani's motto: life wasn't going to hand you lemons, eggplant, a liter bucket of milk, or a *matka* of water. If you wanted anything, you had to go after it.

Being around Naani my uncle, and to some extent my parents shaped my way of thinking at a young age. However, as I grew up in America, that started to change. I started buying into the traditional "there's a better tomorrow" mentality, and suddenly I was at life's mercy. I waited for things to happen to me or for me, waited for a

CHAPTER 5: THE BETTER TOMORROW IS NOT COMING; IT'S ALL ON YOU

certain person to descend into my life and make things better, which brings us to the brutal truths.

Number one: no fairy godmother is going to fox-trot into your life and brandish a better tomorrow for you on a golden platter. Stop waiting—it's not going to happen.

Number two: forget the fairy godmother, but also hold no expectations from anyone else to "save" you from life. Whether you're miserable in your job, unhappy with your body, or tired of your relationship with your significant other … that person is not coming.

Both of those points carry one message: nothing and no one external will make your life better.

Let's elaborate.

As with a lot of people, there was a time in my life when I felt helpless. If you don't believe me, refer to chapter 1. I fell into the trap of waiting, hoping, praying for some magical, transformational event to turn life around for me in incredible ways. I waited for things to change with my parents. I waited for my marriage to get better or for me to have a positive change of heart. I waited and waited.

You can probably relate. People live for that one day when their problems will disappear or life will suddenly be okay, tolerable, manageable. The one day their weight will fall off and they'll suddenly squeeze into their high school jeans, or a company president will reach out and offer them their dream job, or

One person can save you, and they're staring at you in the mirror every damn day you're sulking in wait.

their kids will transform into champion spellers who compete in the national spelling bee (or at least learn to put the dishes away).

The magical, transformational day I was waiting for just never came for me. In fact the best day of my life was the day I realized it was never going to come. This whole notion of a better tomorrow sashaying its way into life was a hoax. The quicker we made peace with that, the more productive we could be.

The alternative—false hope—was unproductive; it placed the power of your life outside your reach. I no longer fall prey to that mindset anymore—and I refused to let my employees either. I flat out tell them that a better tomorrow is *not* about to float through the doors. That their best friend, spouse, or parents cannot save them. One person can save you, and they're staring at you in the mirror every damn day you're sulking in wait.

Control It, Own It

Here's why embracing this truth is important: because every day that you play the waiting game is a day you're disempowering yourself from taking control. And it's another day you're releasing that control to an unknown nonexistent source. Instead of being proactive, you're waiting, idle. In your stagnancy, you're sure to vacuum up anxiety as you lie in wait for that magical tomorrow.

That nonsense needs to stop before it sucks the life right out of you.

The ASA Way doesn't wait for tomorrow to happen. Instead it follows the practices of a wise woman who knew way more than she probably ever gave herself credit for: my naani. We seize control, we take action, we set goals, we take charge.

And goal setting and tracking is the perfect way to snatch that control back from that magical person or day or moment you're waiting for.

Let me give you a prime example of what taking control means. When it comes to evaluations or feedback at my firm, I hold conversations with employees throughout the year—not just during annual reviews at year-end. From a development standpoint, I've found year-end reviews to be an utter waste. You're sitting across from someone, recapping an entire year that's already escaped your clutches, rehashing missed opportunities that can no longer be repossessed and discussing what you could have, should have, would have done. There's no shot at corrective behavior, which only leads to resentment on all sides. Your manager is upset at what you didn't achieve, and you're pissed that you can't do anything about it now. Why wait until it's too late to discuss how far off the mark the progress is?

Before we go further, let me just get this out of my system really quickly: the words *review* and *evaluation* make me choke a little. Because they're not exactly the right words to describe what happens in these meetings. The word *review* might suggest me sitting there, pointing out all the wonderful and terrible things employees have done. But that couldn't be further from the truth. When I'm with employees, we're not just talking performance metrics—because while those are important, they're not the be-all and end-all of everything. Sure, we talk about areas of opportunity, reasons they may have missed out on the big bonus, or why they might be off mark for a salary bump.

But as part of the ASA program, quarterly evaluations are a dialogue where everyone is talking and sharing. They're a time to set both professional *and* personal goals—because remember, personal and professional lives spill into each other.

The ASA Way is about probing, understanding, and learning what's going on with your people. Of course, you can respect people's boundaries by prefacing these talks by saying, "Hey, I understand if you don't want to go into details about your personal life. But if you could help me understand where you're coming from, I can help you get to a better place."

Create a platform where your employees feel safe enough to share information like that.

I lead these conversations by asking associates to reflect on the previous quarter and have an honest discussion about what they've accomplished and areas where they feel they fell short with goals, personal and professional.

Maybe you're feeling a little confused right now. You might be thinking, *Okay, I get it. Personal and professional lives spill into each other, but how do employees' personal goals have any relation to work performance—and why the hell are you discussing those with your employees?*

Imagine this. You want to own your own home. It's been your dream for the longest time, and you're tired of renting the apartment below Miss Agatha, who tap dances to *American Idol* every evening. Your personal goal is to move the hell out and buy your own place, where you're not tossing money down the trash receptacle every month paying rent. Your dream comes true, and you move into your own place. Are you going to come to work upset or pumped up? Are you going to be grouchy or excited when you sit at your desk, sipping coffee?

The thing about personal goals is when you achieve them, you start feeling better about yourself. You're more positive, energetic, empowered, which feeds into your productivity at work. Here's the other thing: it's rare to meet people who meet their metrics performance-wise but don't make any meaningful strides in their personal lives. If you're not making strides personally, you'll stop making them professionally. And I don't want that to happen with me or my associates.

Quarterly reviews are a chance for me to have a real conversation with my team—not too frequently, to the point where I'm constantly in their bubble, but frequent enough to where I don't lose sight of what's going on with them. These quarterly meetings also give me a glimpse into my employees' lives and what they're going through. That matters, because we're not robots. Setting goals with your employees while being blindfolded about what's going on in their personal lives is like pushing them off a mountain while they're struggling to find their parachute: you're setting them up for failure.

What if an employee has a sick child or has a family member on life support or is in the thick of a divorce? And here you are, setting sky-high goals for them? You're not doing either of you, not to mention the client, any favors, unless your definition of *favor* means giving you both a reason to have excessive anxiety when those goals aren't achieved.

I set goals based on where I see potential *but* within the context of putting each employee in the best position to succeed. That's your job as an employer. Just like it's the job of any coach: to place the team in the best position to succeed on every play.

Once we map out what goals they've conquered from the previous quarter, we follow it up by setting more aggressive goals for the next one, as long as I'm confident they're in a healthy headspace.

Let's get back to the "better tomorrow" part of this chapter. You do have a shot at a better tomorrow. There could be a brighter, better future ahead of you. And the key to that future is setting realistic goals and expectations both personally and professionally. Once you start jumping on those goals, you'll gain more control over your life. You'll see better results. You *will* be rescued. But it will be all thanks to you, no one else.

The beauty of it is that control is addictive. The more in charge you feel of your life, the more you'll believe that you *can* do something about the challenges and obstacles around you every day, and the more confident you'll grow in your skills and capability to take authority over your life versus waiting for somebody else to come swooping in to fix your problems.

That's incredibly empowering, because at the end of the day, if you succeed, that success is on you. And if you don't succeed, it's still on you. The onus of your life falls on your shoulders, and the faster you realize you're holding the reins, the faster you rise to a spectacular tomorrow.

Now imagine the reverse. Ten years from now, you could either take the above approach and acknowledge responsibility for your life, or you could sob into your pillow and curse the world to damnation, blaming your parents and spouse and dog for all of life's woes. You choose.

Now let's go beyond that a bit.

When we talk about a better tomorrow, we're actually talking in terms of today. Before you go cross-eyed and scratch your head, let me explain.

Tomorrow is not something that's objectively measurable, but today is. So say if you set a goal to learn how to ride a bike (because your parents never taught you—but hey, we're not blaming anyone, because you're taking charge of you, remember?). You may hope that at some point in the future, like tomorrow, you'll master the technique. But the best way to make that happen is to focus on today. If you hit a goal every single day—say the first day's goal is to get on a bike, the next goal is to learn how to pedal, then to remove the training wheels—those collective efforts add up over time. At the end of the month, you can sure as hell bet you'll be riding that bike—shit, you might be flying on it or even popping a wheelie.

Taking Responsibility Like a Pro

Unfortunately, like in every other business, I've had to let people go. Why? Because they refuse to take accountability for their lives. Honestly speaking, I've never regretted it. Because my first reaction is to accommodate, accommodate, accommodate. I work to understand employees on a personal level. I listen. I empathize. I give them breathing room and cut them slack. So if despite those efforts they refuse to wake up, see what's happening with their lives, and learn to take accountability just because it's easier to blame someone else or think their life is beyond their control, I have no qualms about cutting them loose.

Unfortunately, the world is full of people just like this. No matter what you tell or teach them, they'll blame their flaws, their setbacks, their problems, their life on someone or something else. When that mindset becomes their default, however, I know that no matter what I do or what resources I provide, they'll

Today (and by default, tomorrow) is a choice. You either choose to adapt and make it yours or you choose not to.

never take accountability and realize they're holding the damned reins. That's when I know we've come to the end of the road—because you can only help people to the extent they're willing to be helped.

Here's what you need to know to avoid falling into the trap of victimizing yourself: understand that today (and by default, tomorrow) is a choice. You either choose to adapt and make it yours or you choose not to. What you choose is entirely your prerogative—and the subsequent results are also on you.

The Challenges of Accountability

Make no mistake, holding yourself accountable is so damned hard. At any given moment on any given day, you have a million excuses to fail. And the pandemic has only exacerbated the problem. Maybe you have a child who's being virtually schooled, or maybe your spouse is in the other room on calls, constantly disrupting your focus. It's easier than ever to toss in the towel and say, *Hell, I didn't meet this deadline or goal because of [insert external factor of your choice here].*

But all that means is that you have to be that much more focused, persistent, resilient in adopting a mindset that screams, *No matter what the hell's going on around me, I'm moving the fuck ahead.* Get ear plugs, create a schedule, get help from a family member or paid help. There are a thousand solutions for every problem—you just have to be willing to seek and pursue them.

One of my best employees, who is motivated to a fault, called me one day. She's a model employee: high achiever, go-getter, super energetic to the point that it's easy to assume she's never had a bad day her entire life. Every day she shows up to work, and every day she kills it. I mean slays.

"Hey, Bossman," she said when I answered. "I need a couple of days off. I feel bad asking, but lately I just can't make it out of bed."

I paused, surprised. Never in an eon would I have imagined anything was even going on with her. How could it have been that this chipper woman who was kicking ass at work had been struggling internally?

"Let's dissect for a bit," I said to her.

For the next hour or so, we talked, going deeper into her struggles. It was clear she'd been silently enduring personal challenges. Once we identified them, we turned to pinpointing solutions. How could she still stay in control and maintain ownership of what was happening to her? She pondered that question for a bit.

"No one's coming to save you," I told her as I waited for her to respond. "So let's figure out what we can do to help you save yourself."

Now, I'm not heartless. As I was saying that to her, I was also feeling empathetic. Because truth be told, I'd been feeling the same way, especially after the pandemic. I felt more beat up than ever, and keeping my body and mind going every single day, especially with travel and family in the mix, was a struggle. But I knew that just meant I had to be more dedicated to taking greater control over the things I could, like prioritizing my health and well-being.

I shared my personal routine with her (more about that in chapter 7). And then I asked her to share hers both prior to COVID-19 and now. Surprisingly but not surprisingly, it hadn't changed.

"You can't have the same routine you did before," I told her. "Life has changed, so why haven't your daily practices?"

Maybe going to the gym would have delivered the right focus and energy to her before, but now it wasn't going to cut it. Despite the regular workout sessions, her mind and body were still fighting to shut down—because the energy and benefits she drew from her routine were no longer sufficient in subduing her daily stresses, which had increased the past year. As such, I advised her to take a couple of days off, paid leave, and retreat to a place where she can decompress, reflect, and reenergize. She was grateful not only for the offer of paid time off but also my empathy and candid advice.

Here's what we all have to understand from that anecdote. When COVID-19 hit, people were in survival mode. We quarantined, held dear to our loved ones, and cherished time with our kids and families, pulling out board games and puzzles. Initially, the change was exciting, even welcome. But the effects of being cooped up in ways we're not used to are manifesting now. People are visibly showing and feeling the stresses of our new norm.

For example, now when I'm squeezed in next to someone on a plane, I'm noticing every little thing they're doing and sound they're making. Are they blowing their nose? Was that a cough? And oh my God, don't they dare fucking sneeze on me.

Pre-COVID-19, if you sneezed, you got a *bless you* and maybe a polite smile. Now if you sneeze, you get a death look, or someone goes screaming in the other direction. We're stressed about things we never used to think about twice before.

Now the moment someone coughs or sneezes, you have a million thoughts shooting subliminally through your mind at lightning speed: What if they have COVID-19? What if I wake up sick? What do I do with my child? Should I quarantine?

This anxiety takes a toll on your mind and body, which means you've got to amplify your level of self-care. Employers have to be more empathetic.

Let's talk about that for a moment. I get that as an employer, it's hard, because a lot of your focus is still on your bottom line—or worst-case scenario, trying to stay in business. After all, you won't have any employees to care for or worry about if you go out of business.

I get it. It's exhausting being an employer today, because not only am I worried about the organization, its finances, and my clients, but I'm also tuned in to stories every single day of what my employees are going through, which can become mentally draining when you're trying to make sure you're taking care of everyone the best you can while also taking care of yourself and your family. Add to that the fact that every minute decision I make will impact every one of them and possibly their families, and my stress levels become amplified times a thousand.

But the goal is to find a good median between managing your business concerns and keeping the well-being of your employees front and center. A part of that is helping them keep focus and maintain control by goal setting.

Just like the climate around us changes socially, economically, and physically every year, so should the goals you set for your employees to help them take control of their lives and their success, which I promise will lead to your own success.

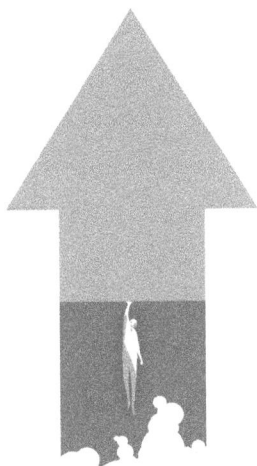

CHAPTER 6

Wake Up in Beast Mode!

NAANI'S DAY ALWAYS STARTED the night before. Every night, she'd lay out her sari for the next morning, pressed and clean; the water containers stood sentry across the door; breakfast ingredients lined the tiny kitchen space near the sink. She'd wake up while the sun was still shrugging off its sleep haze and read scripture from the Quran that sat at her bedside. By the time the sun rose over the horizon, water and milk would be collected for the day, and breakfast would be ready; the kitchen would be spotless.

Every part of Naani's day was preplanned down to the most infinitesimal detail. She was a creature of routine, and her prep work made the most efficient use of her day at a period and in a country where efficiency was essential.

I believe she practiced routine for two reasons. One, she realized how integral it was to seize control of the day (refer to chapter 5!). "You cannot control what's going to happen to you, Shuaib," she'd often say. "But you can control how you respond and react to it."

Two, electricity was scarce. We enjoyed this luxury only a limited amount of time each day, so every tick of the clock was a reminder that we could be cloaked in darkness at any moment, which forced us to scramble and make the most of our time with it. Same with water and heat—sometimes you had it and sometimes you didn't. So when luck was shining, we sure as hell made the most of it, boiling water, cooking, showering, and washing clothes at warp speed.

> **Whether you're an organization or individual, success comes from doing things, repeatedly, over and over again like a crazy person.**

The last chapter served a rude awakening on a cold platter: the life-altering moment we've all been waiting for isn't coming. Success works the same; it doesn't happen by chance. There is no single big moment when success can be turned on or off like a light switch. Whether you're an organization or individual, success comes from doing things, repeatedly, over and over again like a crazy person. I get it—there's nothing sexy about the little things. They're mundane, grueling. But it's those very things that compile over time and land you the big dreams.

Unfortunately, many people don't get to that level of success, because doing cumbersome things repeatedly is boring as fuck and a hell of a commitment. There's nothing sexy about the little things, but it's those things that compile over time to get you the level of success you want to achieve. Do you think Michael Jordan was born shooting hoops? You think he understood strategy, position, and defense from the moment he stopped sucking from a sippy cup? Often I devour biographies and stories about top-performing athletes, my all-time favorite author being Tim Grover, personal trainer to legends like Jordan and Bryant.

His writing describes the tedious, often mundane routines of some of the most legendary athletes of all time, not just on game day but every day, to ensure optimal nourishment of their minds and bodies. For example, in his recounting of Jordan's game-day routine, he describes the player's pregame meals, attire selections, and car wash regimen prior to arriving at the arena. That man never showed up to the arena without a squeaky-clean ride. And once he arrived, he had a strict sequence in which he put on his uniform. There was no *oh, here are my socks, let's toss those on first—oh, I see my shorts there, let me get those on next.* Jordan had a precise, meticulous order. Before every game, he'd pull out a brand-spanking-new pair of shoes straight out of a crisp box and lace them up himself—no help accepted from an equipment manager or helpful soul who offered to do the polite thing and lace them up for him. Tying those shoes with his own two hands put him in the right mindset: calmed him and bolstered his mood right before the game.

As an organization or employee, your daily routine should be as purposeful as Jordan's. I dare you to steal from him and get a head start on your day through an intentional routine that kicks off way before it's time to put your game face on. In fact, do as Naani did and as I now do, and start your preparations the night before. That's a lot more intentional than waking up to a blaring alarm, rubbing sleep crust from your, eyes and thinking, *Aw, hell, let's see what today drags in.* That mindset is reactionary, whereas routine is preplanned, controlled.

Every success is a process, and every process comprises baby steps, often tedious ones.

Let's talk about the best, most ingenious board game in the world: Monopoly. I've always been a Monopoly lover to the point where I could binge play for hours without blinking or remembering to eat. What I enjoy most about it is that it relates directly to how success works.

When you're gliding those cool metal pieces across the board, you have a single aim: to purchase properties of the same color (preferably the blues!) so you can build a hotel and charge the pants off anyone who lands on them. The beauty of it is, you can't build a hotel if you have just one house or even the majority of them. You have to have all four houses before you earn the right to plop down a hotel and smirk as players pray while they roll the dice.

Success works the same. To achieve your end goal, you have to claim victory in the baby steps, practicing patience, consistency, and dedication, before shit goes buck wild in an incredible way, and next thing you know, you're singing on the moon.

Any growth, even the growth of a firm or business, doesn't happen overnight. It happens because you do the little things that add up to the big successes: establishing core values, executing decisions within those values, staying consistent as an organization, etc. Do that over and over again every day, day in, day out, week after week, and that's when you see growth.

Every Day Is Game Day

I get it. Employees are different from professional athletes. Sure, you don't get paid millions to toss a ball to near precision, but you also don't get an off-season. Your game day is every single fucking day. But that only means your routine has to be your focus every single day.

What routine is best for you? Now we're getting personal. Because routines are so damned personal—they have to be, because they have to work for *you*. You can look at your sister's, your neighbor's, or even your spouse's for inspiration, but yours has to be your own blueprint. If you had one before COVID-19, scratch that shit and throw it away. I can almost bet you my Monopoly board that it's not going to work for you anymore. The world has changed immeasurably since then, and like I said in the last chapter, so should your routine.

If you're itching to know what a strong routine looks like, I don't mind sharing mine with you. In fact I shared it with my team just recently, most of them having no earthly idea how involved it was (or that I even had one).

But that's the thing about being front and center; your actions look effortless, easy to spectators. When Jordan was on the court, he'd cross it, get into position, twist, aim, fire, and the ball would fly into the hoop. Simple.

But books like Grover's are a reality check, shedding light on the ceaseless effort athletes put into their minds and bodies to get them to work the way they do. That's similar to how employees view their leaders. It wasn't until I unveiled my routine that I saw a few eyes nearly pop out of their sockets.

Let me be clear. Before COVID-19, my routine was pretty meh. I set out my clothes the night before, woke up the next morning, worked out, showered, went to work, came home, had dinner, and said hello to my bed. Right before COVID-19 hit, I was already reevaluating this routine, because its fizz was wearing off: it didn't feel empowering to me anymore. Today, I've amped it up ... a lot.

In fact my routine is no longer just a daily routine but also has weekly, monthly, quarterly, and annual practices built into it. In case you're curious, here's a brief glimpse.

Shuaib's Personal Routine

I admired Naani's efficiency, so I follow her practice of prepping the night before. I choose my clothes for my workout and work; match my tie, socks, belt, watch, and shoes; and pack my briefcase in the order that I'll unpack it so I don't make a mess tossing things back and forth in search of something. In my kitchen, my breakfast ingredients are fully laid out. My car is autoprogrammed to rev up at a certain time and be set to an optimal temperature, and my coffee is preordered and ready for pick up the same time every day. I also preorder my meals so I know exactly what I'll be consuming and don't get tempted to grab something unhealthy on a whim or in haste.

When I wake up, it's never to a blaring alarm. Those damned alarms are a health hazard and scare me half to death. Instead, I've programmed meditation sounds into my phone. Peaceful strains first thing in the morning put my mind at ease, which is so much better than waking up scared shitless.

Then comes my gratitude journal. This isn't an actual physical journal but one I have on my phone where I can jot down five things I'm grateful for each day. Sometimes those things repeat from day to day, and sometimes they're fresh thoughts. Being grateful and starting off on a positive note first thing in the morning puts me in a good headspace the rest of the day.

Next, I write down an intention, or what I want to accomplish, for the day. Some days the intention is more involved than other days. But articulating an intention is important for me, because I keep returning to it throughout the day to keep me focused on my goals. As the day progresses, it can take many unexpected turns that sidetrack you, putting you in a funk and dragging you out of routine. If you've ever had a flat tire, a sick child, or an accident on your way to work, you know exactly what I mean.

The other crucial component of my morning is practicing mindful meditation. Basically, this type of meditation encourages a state of mind where you simply accept—not react to—whatever it is you're feeling. By doing this, you're training your mind to be curious about emotions, not letting them control you or your reactions.

Leaders are responsible for hundreds of decisions that impact many people, which can be mentally taxing. Because energy starts in your head and ends there too, everything you do from working out to going to sleep affects your mental health, so I've made it a point to focus on my mind by incorporating self-talk and positive affirmations into my meditation routine.

When you let your head talk, its default is to drag you toward negative thoughts, creating a disempowering situation where you're not in control and resort to blaming people, things, or situations. You might curse a nail on the road for your flat tire. You might get angry at your spouse for bringing home a viral bug they passed to your child. All of a sudden, you're trapped in the negative energy of your own mind. Self-talk redirects your thoughts in a positive direction.

Affirming positive thoughts also rewires your mind so that its default is positivity, not negativity. Practice it enough, and you can physiologically change the neural pathways of your brain. From experience, I can tell you rewiring your mind through positive self-talk creeps into your professional and personal dealings in awesome ways.

After practicing positive affirmations for a while, I started responding differently to situations. For instance, if a client hired another firm,

I used to take it personally, thinking maybe it was because of a short-coming in me. But now that's no longer my instinctive reaction. Now I think, *Hey, maybe that firm was a better fit for them. Great.*

Rewiring your mind through positive self-talk creeps into your professional and personal dealings in awesome ways.

After I take care of my mind, I focus on taking care of my body by hitting the gym (more about that in the next chapter) at least five to six days a week. Then comes coffee and getting dressed for work. That's my daily routine before the clock hits 8:00 a.m. The rest of my routine comprises the following:

WEEKLY

→ I take vitamin B$_{12}$ shots weekly to make sure I have sustained energy and mental clarity to last the workweek.

TWICE A MONTH

→ I take immunity boosters through IV therapy, which injects vitamins, minerals, and detoxification components through my bloodstream to protect me against colds and viruses when I travel. Given that I am exposed to airplanes, germ-infested airports, and hotels, this is a must!

→ My body takes a beating from continuous travel, so I also get massages to relax and alleviate stress and muscle fatigue.

→ I schedule cold therapy to fight internal inflammation and keep focus (there's a ton of cool literature on cold therapy, so read up on it).

MONTHLY

→ I donate blood to remove toxins from my bloodstream.

QUARTERLY

→ I get a blood panel to measure my levels and ensure everything is where it should be. If not, I work with my doctor to devise a medical plan. Because everything in your body is related— and if any part of your body is off, your entire being will be off.

→ I choose a book to read. Usually I'll carve out reading time in the morning every day, right before I hit the gym. If a particular day or week is particularly hectic, I make sure I have an audible version as a backup so I can listen to it on my way to the gym. Even a few pages give me infinite inspiration first thing in the morning, keeping me pumped and energized throughout the day.

Obviously I'm not telling you or my employees to go out and adopt this routine. It's pretty fucking intense. But I shared it with them because leadership comes through action, not words. It was important for my team to see that I was practicing what I preached so I could reinforce an environment where employees felt encouraged to take care of themselves and found comfort in being transparent about things personal to them.

Whatever a good routine looks like for you is what you should adopt. Without routine, all you're doing day in, day out is reacting to your day as it comes at you, with little control over the things that *are* in your power: your mind and body. I bet you anything that being routine oriented versus reactionary will leave you energized and happier at the end of every day, because you'll have accomplished a lot of what you set out to.

Why Have a Routine?

Having a routine helps you remain productive not only in your business life but in your personal life too. When you're out of sync because you're not in routine, sure, it will impact you personally, but it'll impact those around you too, including your colleagues, children, husband, wife, or whomever else you spend your day with. Because that frustrated energy you feel brewing within you when you're not on top of your game eventually oozes out. And if you're a business owner, and your clients pick up on it, you're fucked at a whole new level.

I always argue that the most important person in your life should be you. Many people have trouble digesting that because they think that's a selfish mentality. But it's not. When you board a plane, the flight attendants, during preflight instructions, always tell you to secure your own oxygen mask before helping others—including your children. There's a reason for that. You can only help those around you best when you're strong yourself, both physically and mentally.

Now that we've established the importance of routine on a personal level, let's talk at an organizational level. As an organization, the first, most important thing you can do is to acknowledge the importance of routines. Most organizations are least concerned with what their employees do after they exit the building for the day. That thinking passed its expiration date the moment COVID-19 hit.

If you don't think routine is important, then any resource I ask you to consider providing your employees will come across as pointless to you. Have an honest conversation as an organization about whether or not you truly value routines. And if you do, put resources in place so your employees know you're not spewing empty words.

At my firm, my employees mirror a portion (yes, just a portion!) of my own routine. Because while I can't force people to buy into adopting a personal routine, I can and do make sure there are resources available to them that reflect how serious I am about it.

We kick off with gratitude using the gratitude channel (covered in chapter 4) on our internal software collaboration system. This helps employees start off the day on an optimistic note before the workday begins.

We also have another channel called *intentions*. As an organization, our employees set a joint intention to get ahead of the day, remain purposeful against unexpected stressors, and stay in control of their minds and bodies.

As an organization, we host a quarterly book club called (you guessed it!) the ASA book club, where we select leadership-focused books. Obviously, the book club isn't mandatory, but many of the principles that guide our organization are derived from these books. And engaging your employees in a book club has many benefits. First, employees observe their employer constantly educating and seeking high-thought leadership, which builds your credibility. Second, they're able to read what their boss is reading, which gains them a deeper understanding of the organization and why it operates the way it does. Third, it gives everyone an opportunity to connect. If we're up against an issue, it's nice to be able to say, "Hey, the book we were reading mentions something similar and suggests responding this way."

I've mentioned our annual retreat. At it we host a wellness program emphasizing the importance of a healthy weight and addressing common issues like anxiety, self-doubt, fear, shame, and guilt—everything we lawyers and humans are prone to. Again, these sessions reinforce my commitment to my employees' well-being. Throughout the year, we offer one-on-one, completely confidential consultations with our wellness partners.

I'm big about taking care of my body, so I provide employees a gym membership so they can take care of theirs, too, by establishing a wellness routine.

All of these resources serve one purpose: to encourage people to develop a routine they can stick to. It also underscores the importance we give to routine as an organization. When organizations make these resources available to employees, there's no excuse for people to not better themselves and enhance their quality of life.

This is the kind of environment I envisioned fostering long before I started ASA. One, because it's one I would have loved to be a part of but never was as an employee. Two, because I love the feeling of adding value to people's lives. Three, none of the things I've covered cost a ton of money. For instance, gym memberships can run from ten to twenty bucks a person depending on the gym, so they're not going to put a huge dent in your bank account. However, look at the ROI on these resources, and it's substantial. There are a ton of other benefits associated with everything the ASA Way preaches, which we'll cover in chapter 9.

> **Routines are crucial. Without them, you're like a plastic bag being moved and swayed by the wind.**

For now, you should walk away from this chapter knowing this: routines are crucial. Without them, you're like a plastic bag being moved and swayed by the wind. None of your actions are purposeful—just reactionary. That's not what you should want to be as an individual or organization.

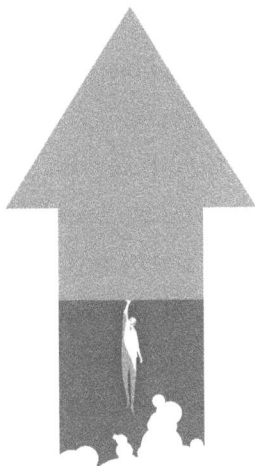

CHAPTER 7

Nourish the Mind and Body to Flourish

EACH MORNING AFTER washing up, the first thing my grandmother did was pull out the Quran from the nook next to her bed and read scripture. She did this religiously (pun intended), without fail, every morning for an hour, regardless of how late she went to sleep or how early she had to be up. I remember her soft voice, full of conviction, reciting Arabic, a language I neither knew nor understood and that sounded a lot like a medley of foreign noises to my ears. Waiting for her to finish felt like a lifetime. "Are you done yet?" I'd always ask. I couldn't understand why anyone would trap themselves in a room for an hour first thing in the morning and go to the trouble of reciting in a language that wasn't their native tongue nor one they understood. But Naani found immense comfort and calmness in prayer.

One rare day, we awoke later than usual, which meant we were already in a scramble to keep up with time. Any later and we could find ourselves at the tail end of the water and milk lines and be lucky if anything were left. And the produce carts, no doubt by the time we made it to them, would be carrying only wilted, subpar misfits. I remember hopping into my clothes before rushing out in search of Naani. "Are you ready, Naani?" I asked, expecting to see her waiting at the door.

But she wasn't there. I went in search of her and found her in her room, reading scripture in her calm, confident tone. "Come on, Naani!" I told her, unable to contain my exasperation. "You already did this yesterday!"

She didn't blink or look up, just continued reading, rocking back and forth, as if I hadn't spoken. When she was done, she closed her prayer book and chuckled. "When you feed your soul first thing in the day, the rest will follow," she told me in our native language, chucking me under the chin. At the time, I was probably six and had no idea what in tarnation she was talking about. "That's great—can we go now?" I said, eager to appease her so we could get on.

Of course, today I know exactly what she was trying to say. By praying every single morning, so uncompromisingly with militant discipline, she was not only feeding her soul but also getting her mind ready by setting the right tone for the day.

For years now, we've heard that it's important to make both the mind and body a priority. But back when the hype started, if you made it to the gym, you got a pat on the back or an, *Oh, good job. That's kinda cool you did that.*

And if you told people you meditated, they'd scratch their heads, wondering if that was code for dealing drugs, or the few who did understand what it was would stereotype you as froufrou and space out.

Today, however, endless research backs regimens focused around both mental and physical health—because both are integral to your being and feed into one another. I like to think of it this way: your body is the shell

Endless research backs regimens focused around both mental and physical health— because both are integral to your being and feed into one another.

or encasement that houses and nurtures you, and your mind is what powers that body to function. Together, they make you *you*! If one or the other is off kilter because you neglect it, you're already functioning at only one half of yourself. That's why giving equal attention to both parts is not optional—it's mandatory. Never once have I met anyone so talented that they can master one aspect, overlook the other, and still sustain success for the long term. If one half of you fails, eventually so do you as a whole.

I know people who are freak athletes—and those who aren't athletes—but still hyperfocused on their physical well-being. These people don't work out a couple of times a week—they work out a couple of times a day. They're also uncompromising about eating right, drinking lots of water, giving the stink eye to carbonated beverages and caffeine, the whole shebang. But often these people overlook keeping their minds healthy too, which more often than not prevents them from progressing in life. The same is true of the reverse. I know people who are at complete Zen in their minds; they're positive, content, relaxed, at peace. They're basically as mentally fit as the other people are physically. But they're also the ones sitting with their pants unzipped in front of the TV, scarfing down twinkies. And so even though they're inspirational, amazing people to be around, they're not as successful as they could be because they're failing one half of themselves.

When it comes to focusing on your mind or body, there's no such thing as choosing one or the other. Both are equally critical. And that means every morning after you're done rubbing eye boogers from your eyes, you should be ready to tank up both those parts of you to the brim, just as you'd tank up your car for the week. Why? Because your mind and body are literally your fuel for both your personal and professional lives. A healthy mind gives you peace and clarity to make the right decisions each day, keeps you grounded, gives you strength, and delivers focus on tackling everyday challenges, whether that means helping Aunt Bertha remember where she left her dentures (again) or figuring out how to wow your boss with a stellar presentation on how your efforts augmented your company's annual revenues.

And of course, we all know the obvious benefits of being physically fit: decreased risk of disease, healthy weight, an optimally functioning body. But there's more: getting the endorphins flowing from a good workout can boost your mood and make you feel good, fostering a positive self-attitude.

So both mind and body are equally important. Do not, I repeat, do not expect to focus on just one and think it will compensate for the other.

Now let's get real. We all know pouring equal amounts of attention on your mind and body is no simple feat. Sometimes shit gets tough. Your spouse might lose their job. A family member might fall sick. A parent might suddenly move in with you and need your support. Life makes it so damned tempting to steer away from these priorities so you can cater to other much more pressing stressors clamoring for your time and attention. When your kid announces that they're moving to Timbuktu and disconnecting from technology, suddenly a sweat session at the gym or getting your chakras aligned seems like some useless shit to be worrying about. But sacrificing either is choosing to sacrifice the most important parts of you! In the chaos of daily life, we don't realize that when the going gets tough is exactly when we need our mind and body to be functioning top of game, all pistons firing. That's why nourishing your mind and your body should become a habit. Notice the word *habit*—make them an uncompromising part of your daily routine. By doing that, you'll be preparing both parts of you for the difficult days to come—that's when you'll reap the true rewards of your investments in you.

I'm always harping to the team about routine and the importance of self-care. Things are going to get tough in life—always, always, always. Expect it. Know it's coming, if it hasn't already. But do not abandon the mental or physical aspects of your routine, if not for anything else then for the simple reason mentioned in the previous chapter: control the shit you can control; two things that fall in that category include what goes in your mouth and what goes into your mind.

Benefits of a Healthy Mind and Body

When you have a sound mind and strong body, as an employee, you'll find yourself to be more focused on whatever you aim to tackle, whether that be your personal goals or your productivity at work. Also, with your mind and body in harmony, you'll feel more optimistic, won't be so easily distracted, and will find yourself able to remain on track with whatever you set out to accomplish each day. How many times did you find yourself in the break room surrounded by other people's drama? It's like being in a high school bathroom (i.e., "You won't believe what happened …"). Having a balanced mind and body serves as a shield, blocking out the unnecessary noise and helping you remain focused. Sure, that's incredible news from a personal standpoint, but it's not so shabby news from an employer standpoint either—think of what your employees could achieve with that kind of focus!

As an employer, you'll also be happy to know that a healthy person means a resilient, happy employee. And when your employees feel happy, that shines through in their interactions with coworkers and clients, which boosts your business, pulling your bottom line up along with it.

As an organization, it's in your best interest to make sure your employees are operating at 100 percent through their bodies and minds.

Here's proof of why: More than once, judges have approached me in the courtroom and said, "You guys are doing something right over at your law firm. Many of the attorneys who come in and out of our courtrooms seem upset, angry, and grumpy. Then you see attorneys from ASA, and they have smiles on their faces, they're prepared, they're professional, and it feels like they're enjoying not only what they do but also what's around them."

I believe the ASA Way, its emphasis on mental and physical health, and its efforts to provide resources to promote well-being in both areas are a large contributing factor to that observation.

Let's hit on the resources part for a moment.

In the previous chapter, we talked about providing resources so your employees feel empowered to develop a routine. And the same holds true when we're talking about promoting well-being. Many employers see the benefits of offering gym discounts and memberships. But if you're skipping out on investing in employee mental health, you're making a grave mistake. Organizations that don't provide resources for mental health in a value-based way are most likely to lose dynamic workers who can't perform at optimal levels because they lack the outlet or resources to manage challenges they're encountering mentally both at work and at home.

Many organizations balk at this and ask, *Now why in the hell would I do that? Why should I spend money, time, and resources on things people can and should be individually responsible for?*

To build a productive team in your organization, you need to build productive, empowered individuals.

My answer to that is, employees won't know with conviction that you care about their well-being—even if you're screaming it from the mountain tops—unless you show them you do. You want your claims to resonate with your employees. You want to come across as sincere. And when you provide resources to your employees instead of painting the walls with statements screaming you care about them, it does just that. It emphasizes your commitment to your values. It shows employees you're sincere in your concern for them. And here's the other thing: to build a productive team in your organization, you need to build productive, empowered individuals. You can't have the level of production you need in today's world without focusing on the individualistic component of people. It's only when healthy individuals come together that they can make a healthy team.

Putting Mind and Body into Practice at ASA

I mentioned that we provide our employees gym memberships. We also have a work-from-home option, which allows our employees flexibility in being able to get in their daily exercise. I like going first thing in the morning, but I know others who find it most calming and effective at night, once the day is over, the kids are in bed, and they're alone with their thoughts. Still others prefer to get those endorphins pumping during the midday slump. I don't care what time of day my employees work out, as long as whatever they choose to do works best for them and will help them commit. By providing a gym membership combined with work flexibility, I've stripped employees of the "I don't have time" excuse. Also, I can say that the organization has done everything in its power to promote its value of employee well-being. It's given them the resources, encouragement, and means to prioritize their health: putting their socks on and pounding the pavement is up to them.

For mental health, our approach is the same. According to the CDC, 40 percent of people claim having mental health or substance use challenges as of June 2020.[4] That's a lot. Sure, a large part of it could be attributed to the pandemic, but there's also the collateral damage resulting from it in the form of uncertainty, anxiety, stress, etc. What can make your organization dynamic is being the one certain thing in an uncertain world.

Our corporate wellness program is available to all employees not only at our annual retreat but also throughout the year, when they can choose to access it anonymously.

---

4   "Mental Health, Substance Use, and Suicidal Ideation During the COVID-19 Pandemic—United States, June 24–30, 2020," CDC, August 14, 2020, https://www.cdc.gov/mmwr/volumes/69/wr/mm6932a1.htm.

Let me say, I like to think I'm a pretty approachable guy, but I understand not everyone might think so. Or they might not feel comfortable discussing personal, sensitive issues with the person responsible for cutting their paychecks. The wellness program gives them an outlet in a private one-on-one setting with a professional counselor whom they can trust and share thoughts with openly.

Again, our organization provides the resources, but the onus falls on our employees to avail themselves to these resources. In the meantime, you can revel in the satisfaction that you've put action to making your values real for your employees and organization. (Remember, when you put your values to action, you're creating a culture!)

And just as real will be the results you see in your bottom line, the ambition you see in your employees, and the overall positivity you see exuding from your staff.

Reflecting Inward

Here's an important disclaimer: if you yourself are an organizational leader, you really need to get your shit together in your own mind and body before you decide to help others in that avenue. You can't help others or serve as motivation if you aren't helping yourself first. Imagine preaching physical fitness when every day you're seen scarfing down Snickers bars and Big Macs and haven't seen a gym since 1992. Or imagine touting mental health when you show up grouchy, upset, or anxious to work most of the time. You can't expect your employees to understand the importance of nourishing their minds and bodies when you, the person preaching it, don't show commitment to that philosophy.

Determining Resources

Of course, once you put physical and mental resources into play at your organization, don't just dust off your shoulders and lean back.

Although the world of yesterday no longer exists, you can always prepare for tomorrow.

Change is the name of the game. Keep evaluating your employees' needs and modifying the resources you offer—because times change, and so will the resources your staff requires to function at their best. Observe what's happening in your workforce, industry, society, or even the world and see how that might be affecting your employees. Because although the world of yesterday no longer exists, you can always prepare for tomorrow.

When we allocate resources at our firm, the ASA Way approach doesn't look first at balance sheets, see what's left over, and figure out what we can squeeze into the available budget. I look at the issues surrounding employees today and prioritize what items from a resource aspect would alleviate those issues. That's when the balance sheet comes out and I ask myself, Okay, how can we make this happen?

The other thing is, I'm not just tossing resources at employees and saying, *Here ya go, use this.* We say, *Hey, would you give this a shot and provide some feedback to us, please? What can we tweak? We want to make sure this is working the best way it possibly can for you.*

Trust me, it works. People want to give feedback. We've modified our programs so many times based on this very feedback.

Once you get in the hang of garnering feedback, making changes, and reevaluating resources, you're well on your way to creating an empowered organization driven by empowered employees. Then all you have to do is … stick to everything we've talked about. We'll cover that next.

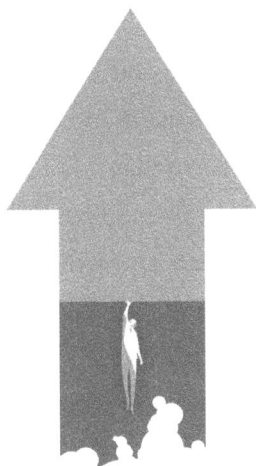

CHAPTER 8

Committing to Commitment

I'VE HIT ROCK BOTTOM several times in my life. During my fallout with my parents, my attempted suicide in college, and my divorce. No matter how fast I scrambled to escape trouble, it seemed like something worse was always waiting around the corner. I became so used to the view at rock bottom that the moment life began to inch upward, I was always wary, waiting for the next plummet.

At some point after my divorce, I began analyzing my life choices and beliefs. It occurred to me then that my actions were inconsistent with those beliefs. I don't mean everyday actions like brushing my teeth or taking out the trash. I'm talking about actions that defined who I was and my true purpose and making a heartfelt commitment to those.

Until that point, any success I'd achieved in my life had been brief and sporadic. If I wanted any chance at lasting success in life, I knew I needed to find out what I stood for and commit to that.

Similarly, if you're an individual or an organization that chooses the ASA Way, you've got to be committed to your beliefs and what you're all about, no matter whether, when, or how hard the shit hits the fan; you have to stay committed to your ASA game plan.

Let's define commitment for a second. When we're talking about committing, we're talking about several things. We're not just talking about having a conversation in your mind saying, *Hey, no matter what happens around here, we're going to stick to the ASA Way, damnit.* It's not as simple as that. Committing encompasses several components and includes a few steps.

Back to Authenticity

For an organization, having an honest conversation about who you are (refer to chapter 3 on authenticity) is where it starts. Once you know yourself, understand how you can be better, and know which principles you want to incorporate into your culture, the question then becomes, As an organization, how do we go about committing to all of those brilliant thoughts?

Let me say that again in different words, because it's worth emphasizing: The very first thing you should do before you even consider rolling out the ASA Way is to make sure you're being authentic in your approach and what you want to offer employees.

For years and years, your organization has been hardwired to think a certain way. And your employees have been part of that hardwiring in a workforce that's a broadscale reflection of your organization's mindset. For eons, your employees have been convinced that their personal lives need to stay separate from their professional ones. That whatever happens to them outside the corporate walls is not the organization's problem and shouldn't affect work. That the organization is only concerned about work performance and wants them to leave their personal baggage at home.

Now all of a sudden, you're trying to reverse that ideology and roll out an approach that's inconsistent with the norm; that's no small feat.

Be very honest with your employees about why you're even attempting to change your philosophy at this point in your organization's existence, because

The very first thing you should do before you even consider rolling out the ASA Way is to make sure you're being authentic in your approach and what you want to offer employees.

otherwise your hidden propaganda will shine through your words and actions.

Here's what I mean. If you go in there talking about adopting the ASA Way, and you're spewing ROI, balance sheet, and P&L statement lingo, your employees are going to shut you down in a heartbeat. You'll see their eyes glaze over and maybe roll into the back of their heads. You know and I know that's not the type of talk that's going to buy them into the program. I'm not saying those things aren't important. Of course they are. They're just not the right reasons to be giving your employees. Think about why you're doing what you're doing and how it benefits your employees—and talk to them about that!

Also, get used to being vulnerable. Sounds odd and maybe a bit counterintuitive, I know. After all, as a bossperson, your instinct is to be the brave, fearless leader. But vulnerability is so important when you're attempting a psychological overhaul of your organization. Think about it. You're going in front of a crowd of associates, preaching about personal life feeding into professional, expecting these associates to buy into this ideology and share their personal lives with you. When your spiel is over, you can't clam up, sit down, fold your arms, and zip your lips on your own woes. You can't expect employees to open up when you don't. You yourself have to set the precedent.

So what does it mean to be authentic but also vulnerable? For example, it could look something like this: You could explain to associates that your reason for adopting the ASA Way is that, as an executive, you understand the challenges of loving your career but also the struggles of juggling a family alongside it. And you've experienced firsthand the adverse impacts on both productivity and morale when you've tried to separate and balance both in your own role as a leader. Then offer examples of your personal experiences.

That's personal. That's authentic. That's vulnerable.

In my meetings, I keep vulnerability top of mind. When I'm doing mental check-ins every quarter with employees, I usually lead off by discussing my vulnerabilities, almost instantly creating an atmosphere of acceptance. And this is intentional. By doing that, I'm communicating the message, *Guys, I trust you with what I've just shared about myself. You can trust me too.*

Employees are human beings. They understand that no one, including an organization, is flawless. And they'd appreciate and respect you much more for acknowledging your shortcomings than trying to conceal them. That's how people feel they can trust and relate to you.

If you can't find anything personal to say about why you're adopting the ASA Way, you should pause right here. Because more than likely this is not the right approach for you.

Location, Location, Location

Next is location. Think about where you're going to physically conduct this conversation. Are you going to be sitting in a boardroom? Or host a Zoom meeting? Or are you planning on gathering outdoors at a local campground? Or maybe for an informal happy hour?

Where the conversation takes place is just as important as how it takes place. If you're sitting in the same boardroom where you've spewed serious robotic, corporate babble a gazillion times before, that space already is already riddled with a preexisting ambiance and expectation that's engrained in your employees' minds. You can't enter a space that holds connotations of formal, stiff-collared conversations and expect people to feel at ease discussing something as personal as feelings, what it's like to be human, and the shit that's going on in their personal lives. It won't resonate; you're in a conventional setting addressing a very unconventional concept.

Changing the Status Quo

Lastly, adopting the ASA Way, in many cases, will mean modifying or even completely overhauling your previous corporate approach to reflect your commitment to treating employees like people who are significant beyond your bottom line.

For instance, you might change a long-standing process or provide resources that align with the ASA Way. Your words need to match your actions. Most corporations are great at talking but suck at doing. But when an organization commits resources and dollars to what it preaches, it emits a powerful message to the workforce.

For example, if you say you care about employees' health, you could increase health insurance contributions to cover more expenses on their behalf, understanding that in the midst of a pandemic, people are going to be more reliant than ever on healthcare professionals. Or maybe you encourage remote work to help associates focus time on their families.

These actions reemphasize and corroborate your commitment to employees' personal empowerment, which will feed into their professional successes.

Resisting the Resistance

You can bet your life there will be times your organization's commitment to the ASA Way will be put to the test. For instance, you might have a tough fiscal year at some point. How will you respond? Will you start reprimanding employees for not producing? Lay off workers? Pull back resources? Every decision you make after your public buy-in to the ASA Way is going to be scrutinized by employees under a magnifying glass to determine how serious you are about your commitment. You lie, you fry. So you better be prepared to stick to your guns through and through. What defines an organization, much like people, is not how you operate when things are going well but how you respond in times of adversity. People will always remember how you responded when they needed you the most.

Earlier, I shared how because of the shutdown, we had a dour financial year and how productivity took a hit. We could have looked at our bottom line and said, eh, numbers aren't so great. We're not doing bonuses this year, or we're cutting back on salaries, or we're going to furlough some workers. Obviously, we didn't do any of those things, because they didn't fit into our values or company culture.

Alternatively, we sat down with employees to unveil some of the challenges they were facing, asked them to share personal struggles, and determined how we could help. And we knew they were facing challenges, because you don't go from having a team of great producers to all of a sudden seeing productivity dip for no damn reason. Something was up.

We were spot on. The pandemic was taking a toll on people personally and, as a result, professionally. This was the time to step up and prove our commitment to prioritizing our employees.

We shut down the office for a day, took the staff out for a spa day, and then went out to dinner. Doesn't sound like those would have had a huge impact on anything, I know. But after just that one day of R&R, believe it or not, productivity skyrocketed. And it's because employees saw firsthand that this firm was not one of those that would leave them high and dry. It was not going to let them down, and it was prepared to stick by its commitment to its people. And so in turn, these employees worked hard to not let the firm down.

There are going to be times when your organization is chal-

> **To help people, empower them, and care about them takes time and effort. The commitment is not easy. But the results and outcomes are more than worth it.**

lenged. The easy way out is to cut costs. To lay people off. To put people on probation because their productivity is suffering. But to help people, empower them, and care about them takes time and effort. The commitment is not easy. But the results and outcomes are more than worth it.

What Commitment Looks Like

No matter how big or small your organization, everything you do has to align with your commitment. Sometimes that might look like leaving money on the table to avoid buying into something that would go against your commitment. Sometimes it might mean spending more than you want to so you can prove your commitment. Both demonstrate your loyalty to a philosophy you wholeheartedly back.

The one thing I'll say is, don't be a Monday-morning quarterback. In other words, don't do something once to prove your commitment only to revert back to your old ways after a while. That's not how lasting changes are made.

For us, every single year, every single quarter, we implement the things we've committed to implementing to make sure our messaging remains consistent. You can achieve that by incorporating certain practices into your weekly, monthly, quarterly, and annual processes as an organization until they become clockwork.

This is where routine comes in handy. Write down what you'd like to do weekly, monthly, quarterly, and annually to ensure you stay on track. For instance, we do mental check-ins every six months. Annually we do a retreat where we talk about things that have nothing to do with work and everything to do with becoming a better human. These routines help keep us on track with our commitments. The key is consistency—but don't be fooled into thinking you have to do it all alone.

I'm a big believer in delegating tasks and responsibilities so I can be more efficient with my time and my firm's. I rely on a whole team of people to keep me honest and on track. I have a director of operations and attorneys who are team leads and with whom I correspond regularly.

Each of these leaders in their own right is working with their respective teams to make sure we're staying committed to our quarterly and annual tasks. They do check-ins, give me feedback about employees, and work with me to figure out what resources we can offer to those facing challenges.

So when we're rolling out initiatives and wanting to ensure loyalty to our commitments, I have an entire network that has my back.

Full Disclaimer

Adopting the ASA Way is more responsibility than embracing the traditional approach. To be clear, the traditional approach is where you're preoccupied with your bottom line and busy running productivity reports. It's objective. It's measurable. The ASA Way is about promoting productivity and boosting your profits, yes. But in addition to that, it's also about getting to know people at a unique level. It's personable. It's human. I keep my pulse on the happenings of my staff every single day. Sometimes someone loses their mom. Sometimes someone is facing a life crisis.

I stay in the know because, number one, I feel like that's my job. As an owner, it's my responsibility to know my workers inside the organization but also outside of it. Number two, if I know what's happening, I can help. Doesn't matter if they're an attorney, staff member, or office administrator. My efforts prove that although I might have a million things going on at any given time, I'll always take a moment to prioritize them. Third, as an attorney and business owner, it's important for me to know if my employees have things going on before I assign them a case. Putting them in charge of someone else's troubles at a time when they're enduring their own is not only a disservice to that attorney but also to the organization and the client.

Does this level of investment in keeping track of everyone get mentally exhausting? Abso-fucking-lutely.

That's why it's integral for you, as a leader, to master and prioritize your own well-being and health so you can then be that boulder of support for everyone else in your organization—all while empowering them to become a strength in and of themselves, inside and out.

That's why when we talk about our personal empowerment and self-improvement, it's important to do all the things we discussed to nourish our minds and bodies so that we can be available to our employees. Like I said, it's not sufficient to preach. You have to do what you say, live it, practice it, perfect it, day in, day out, so that you can be the best version of yourself for you and your employees.

The Positive Effects

Everything we've talked about so far is time-consuming as all get out. But time is a miniscule sacrifice in the grand scheme of the impact you'll have on people's lives and the results you'll see for your organization. Turnover will be very low. Your clients will be better served. Long term, your workforce will go above and beyond your expectations without you ever having to ask. You'll see the impact on your ROI.

How do I know all this? I know because I've been living and breathing the ASA Way for a long time, and we grew from one firm to two in just five years. But just like any other investment in the world, you have to invest first before you reap the rewards. You might not see them the first month or two or eighteen. But I promise, you'll see them. Especially if you're an organization that's been doing things vastly differently, know that it will take time and a proactive effort to get where you want to be. Just make sure to stick to the ASA Way values and make decisions that reinforce who you are and who you want to be.

How Do You Roll This Out?

When I think about some of the places I've worked, no way in hell would I ever, even with a gun pointed at me, divulge anything personal to my employer. And if one day all of a sudden, an executive came into the room and said he wanted to hear about me and get to know me, my first reaction would be, "Get the hell away." If you can relate, that means that like me, your trust, too, has been breached at some point by an organization. Most corporations are notorious for promoting a corporate, stiff, tight-lipped atmosphere where employees are expected to be robots, not humans. To reverse that ideology is a tough task.

When you're rolling this out as an organization, you're attempting to reestablish trust. You're demonstrating that it's okay to be vulnerable, and you're doing that by setting an example of vulnerability yourself. Remember, it's a top-down approach that starts with you—the leader!

We've talked at length about what commitment means from an organizational perspective. Now let's shift gears to what it means for you as an employee.

Commitment on a Personal Level

In chapter 5, we talked about how the better tomorrow isn't going to fall in your lap and nobody can save your ass but yourself. Your organization can provide resources, venues, and materials you can take advantage of. But as an individual, you are ultimately responsible for staying committed to your own growth and improvement. You have to live every single day committing that, come hell or high water, you'll live by the ASA Way principles day in, day out—without compromise. Commit to the elements of the ASA Way: be authentic, stick to your values, set a routine, take care of your mind and body, etc. To see long-term benefits in both your personal and professional lives, you have to be staunch in your commitment.

Like I said, I'm annoying when it comes to my routine. I don't care where I am—home or out traveling. I stick to it because I know the importance of it and how it changes people and lives. It took me a whole lifetime to understand how important commitment is. But it's fucking hard sometimes, because life is a huge distraction with so many ups and downs. When times get tough, your natural inclination is to say, "Fuck this," and jump ship. That's your default. But if you stick to it

When your organization does things consistently and commits to them, people in the industry, whether they're your partners, vendors, or clients, take notice and recognize you for it.

in those times, that's when you'll see things really start to turn around for you. That's what happened to me. When I made that commitment to take care of myself and follow my beliefs uncompromisingly, creating a game plan that aligned with that goal, that's when I started seeing lasting results.

When your organization does things consistently and commits to them, people in the industry, whether they're your partners, vendors, or clients, take notice and recognize you for it. For example, when people hear ASA Law Group, they understand that we're holistic, that we move cases and close them as quickly as possible, that we're focused on personal and professional development. These messages are out there because we've stuck by and executed on them consistently to the point that they're what we're known for now.

Similarly, if you as an individual commit to that consistency and do it over and over again, people will know what you're about, understand where you're coming from, learn what you stand for, and feel comfortable working and associating with you.

If that consistency is missing, you're not going to have that tangible, lasting success that you want—not just in your personal and professional lives but in any endeavor you attempt. So keep consistent, and watch yourself and your organization grow consistently.

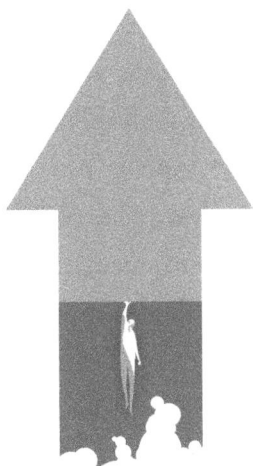

CHAPTER 9

Why Do It?

So. WE'VE LAID OUT this beautiful plan called the ASA Way. You know exactly what it entails. And (I hope) you're eager to jump on the bandwagon and put it to work for you, whether you're an organization or individual. Once you do, what can you expect long term?

I'm glad you asked.

For Individuals

A few chapters ago, I mentioned this, but it's worth repeating. As a human being, when your internal reflects your external and vice versa is when you'll find true, sustained happiness and success—because you're living authentically with no false pretenses or erected facades. I promise you the universe (as bonkers as it may sound) responds to the power of that authenticity—which is what the ASA Way is all about.

You'll find that things will work in your favor to support your goals and vision, making you an unstoppable force in living a life full of purpose. You'll wake up focused and energized from practicing a powerful routine that works for you. And thanks to that routine, your day will be more value based. As you know by now, a lot of what success is isn't about what happens to you but how you respond to what happens. This book gives you the exact tools you need to handle stressors so that you're on the most promising path to that success. And trust me, if you feel like the stressors are out of control, you're not alone. We're all dealing with a shitload more than we ever have before, and the burnout is real as fuck.

But the ASA Way's got your back in kicking burnout butt too!

And of course, the organization you work for also impacts how far you come with the ASA Way. When you choose carefully and work with a company that's aligned with your value system, your work will feel infinitely more fulfilling and adventurous—and your personal life will benefit too. Think about the last time you heard someone say they have fun doing what they do for a living. Having to think hard? I'm not surprised. By making a deliberate decision about committing yourself to an organization, you're taking more ownership and accountability over your life.

It might sound scary, but I promise you the most empowering thought in the universe that you could have is that everything and anything starts and ends with you. Know that you're accountable every single day through every choice you make. That any success attained is due to your efforts, and subsequently, so is any failure.

Finally, after implementing the ASA Way, you'll have the ability to light the way to success for others—at the end of the day, that's what life's all about.

The most empowering thought in the universe that you could have is that everything and anything starts and ends with you.

For Employers

If I had a crystal ball to show you what your future would be like as an employer, I would almost guarantee the first thing I'd tell you is the dramatic change you'll see in your corporate culture. Your employees will feel courageous enough to be vulnerable and authentic at work. I can't tell you how badly that's needed today. Employees are dying to tear down their pseudo exteriors or at least have the choice to do so, especially with everything they're juggling. Being a part of an environment where authenticity isn't encouraged is the most suffocating feeling in the world.

But by instilling a culture that embraces authenticity, you'll be infusing a breath of fresh air into your organization that will help employees improve both personally and professionally. Collectively, those improvements will equate to a team of individuals who are on a mission to carry out the cause of your organization. They'll swap out the mentality that they're working for a company for one where they're working *with* a company—that one word makes a huge difference. In fact, all the difference.

Second, by staying tuned in to employees' personal and professional challenges, you'll have the opportunity to make a significant impact beyond a paycheck in the lives of people, who, yes, happen to also be your employees (remember, be human first!).

Third, you'll start seeing your employees in a very humanistic light, because you'll know them as people first who have personal lives—issues and emotions attached to them. You'll be able to leverage this information to your benefit and theirs by putting them in the best position to succeed, which, let's face it—that's your job. You'll also have the power to be a problem solver by understanding the challenges they're facing and determining which resources you can offer that would help enhance their lives or even propel them out of a current rut. If you do that, your organization is going to shine bright as a fucking star in corporate America, because not many others take the time to not only know people but genuinely help them succeed.

We live in a go-go society where no one's got time for shit. But by weaving these ideologies into your organizational processes to make them inherent to your company, you'll not only make the employees personal to you, you'll make your organization personal to your employees.

I often refer to my team as my second set of children (even though some of them are older than me). For instance, just randomly at any point throughout the day, I'll wonder about my daughter's day at school or how my son is doing with sports practice. It's become the same for my employees. Because I know them almost as intimately as I do my own family, I think about them sporadically throughout the day. I wonder how one employee's father is feeling after falling ill or how another's kid's surgery went. But I don't let those thoughts slip idly by. I take advantage of the moment by shooting a quick text to check in on whomever it is I'm thinking about at the moment.

These actions aren't intentional; they're now automatic and an embedded part of my mindset as a result of practicing the ASA Way. And let me tell you, those seemingly little gestures are huge. That simple message is helping create a bond and fostering a relationship and connection beyond work. People will always remember and appreciate those gestures. It's the right thing to do. It's the human thing to do.

For those perched at the edge of their chairs with their Excel sheets open and calculators at the ready, I've got good news for you. If not for any of the above reasons, know that by doing this, you will see your ROI triple, your productivity increase, and your clients be happier because they're having more positive interactions with your happy employees! Oh, and by the way, your turnover will decrease, and retention will increase.

> **Whether done from the heart (which should be the intent) or the pocketbook, this approach is a win-win no matter how you slice it up.**

Whether done from the heart (which should be the intent) or the pocketbook, this approach is a win-win no matter how you slice it up.

An Eye-Opening Thought

If you need more proof of why adopting the ASA Way is in your organization's best interest, let me share some interesting news with you. According to research, millennials account for about a third of the workforce, and that number is only projected to increase. Most significant is that this generation works, thinks, and operates much differently than any other prior to it.

In fact, I have an interesting story to belabor this point. When our Chicago firm was fairly new, I remember walking in one morning and greeting everyone as I usually do on my way to my desk. Most people were at their workspaces, but one who was usually there first thing in the morning was missing. "Hey," I said, doing a quick skim of the room. "Where's Ms. First-One-In?"

"Here I am!" called a voice. I looked back and forth but didn't see anyone. Then on a hunch, I peeked around her desk and then beneath it. Lo and behold, there she was huddled underneath, music blasting from ear pods and fingers clacking away on a keyboard. She flashed me a smile.

"Hey, Bossman," she said.

"Rock on!" I told her. We fist-bumped.

Sounds like a scene from a movie, I know. But can you in your wildest dreams imagine that ever happening in corporate America—let alone at a law firm—and being perfectly acceptable?!

That's where mindsets need to shift. Keep an open mind, because today's workforce is completely different—and your organization has to be, too, if it wants to not only draw but also retain the best talent from a generation that's well on its way to becoming the dominant presence in our workforce.

I promise I'm not just preaching here. In the back of our office, we have a lounge area replete with dart boards and all sorts of fun activities—because millennials think best on their feet. They're not the kind to sit around and contemplate. Often I'll catch staff strategizing the best angle for a defense while tossing darts or throwing a ball. I rarely ever see them studying at their desk or brooding over a book.

We also jam to music, because silence doesn't seem to suit these young workers. This was an adjustment for me, as someone who was perfectly A-okay with the pin-drop silence so customary of corporate America. However, I realized that everyone works in different ways. Something in the background keeps my staff pumped up and going, so to honor that, we've gotten each associate to submit a playlist, and we choose one to play every day. Sometimes we jam to Drake;

sometimes we belt out country. The point is, I adapted to the new way workers are more productive. (As an aside, listening to the different types of music preferred by each individual clued me in to much more about that person than probably any conversation could.)

That's the workplace now: different personalities, different mindsets, different people. And I'm all game for whatever gets them ticking. Plus, it's way more fun this way.

The bottom line? Be in tune (pun intended!) with your employees, who they are, and what makes them productive and happy—then cater to that. The ASA Way makes the job easy.

Conclusion

OKAY, WE'RE AT THE END of our time together, so time for some straight talk. This very moment in your life, you have a choice: Are you as an individual or employer going to bury your head in the sand and pretend the world is "business as usual" while there's the equivalent of a hailstorm, tsunami, and hurricane swirling around you all at once? Are you going to sit here and pretend like everything is A-okay while we're collectively facing one of the worst pandemics the globe has ever seen?

Or are you going to grab this beast called life by the horns, own what's happening around you, and

Yes, we're in the middle of some hardships. But the good news is that in every hardship, there's opportunity. You just have to search for it.

use what you've learned to create a life-changing, lasting way of empowering workplaces and yourself?

Yes, we're in the middle of some hardships. But the good news is that in every hardship, there's opportunity. You just have to search for it. The opportunity in the here and now is to take complete ownership of our professional and personal lives, strive for a workplace that treats each employee like a human being, develop relationships with employees that traverse the superficial walls of office small talk, and provide resources for employees that help them become the best, most empowered versions of themselves.

Listen, people. The things we've covered in this book aren't rocket science. They're also not financially burdensome. What they require is proactive effort and a pinch of empathy. In other words, do you truly give a shit about your life or your employees' lives?

Do you, as an individual/employee truly want to take ownership of every aspect of your life, hold yourself accountable, and blame no one but yourself?

Think about that. That's incredibly hard. Easier said than done.

How many times have you fallen short and searched for justifications to pin the blame on? I bet you most of the reasons you dredge up are external as opposed to internal. That's gotta go.

You have to be 100 percent committed to looking at yourself in the mirror and saying, *You know what? This one's on me. Here's what I could have done better.* Then move forward and do it!

Employers, tune me out for a minute (if you haven't already). Employees/individuals, this one's for you. I want you to pluck two things from the thoughts floating through your mind space, crumble them up, and toss them into your mental trash receptacle, then burn that shit to ashes and let it float out from your brains into outer space.

One, titles do not matter. Repeat. Titles do not matter. Again. Titles do not matter. Titles don't mean shit in terms of your abilities or who you are as a person. Tell me this. How many times have you been five minutes into a conversation with a partner at a law firm, or a corporate executive, or even the president of an organization and thought to yourself, *How the fuck is this person running their own ship?*

How about the opposite? How many times have you met someone with no title that has more substance than you could have ever imagined? That was my naani. No title, no position, no identity outside of our tiny village. Yet this lady had more character in her pinky nail, more integrity, more wisdom than most people possess in their entire bodies—so much so that I was able to develop not one but two flourishing law practices just by living her example.

The truth is this. Outside of your organization, no one gives two shits about your title. Just because you have a hoity toity title doesn't entitle you to cut in line at the grocery store or sail past red traffic lights.

What matters is the person you are. Because the reward of true success is not what you get but who you become in the journey. (I know, brilliant line, isn't it? Almost tattoo worthy.)

Instead of focusing on titles, focus on you, the person. If you're an authentic, hardworking, honest, empowered individual, I guarantee you there'll be no shortage of opportunities for you, both in your career and in life.

If you're an authentic, hardworking, honest, empowered individual, I guarantee you there'll be no shortage of opportunities for you, both in your career and in life.

Second, stop making career decisions based solely on compensation. That's probably tough advice to swallow, especially when there's so much economic uncertainty. But I promise you compensation will never be enough. Ever. No matter how much you make.

Think about it. Any time you get a raise, you see a small bump in your paycheck, which excites you. Because more money means more opportunities to spend. Maybe you'll buy a bigger house or put a down payment on your dream car. But what happens after that? Maybe you need to dish out a bit more for lawn care, HOA fees, or annual repairs for your home. Maybe your car costs more to maintain than your previous one. This brings you right back to square one—being tight. And so you set out seeking or waiting for the next pay increase.

I get that the days of people being as loyal to companies as they were to their spouses are, let's be honest, long gone. I'm not saying to stay put. All I'm saying is focus on choosing a position or organization that inspires you, moves you, excites you. That will give you a bigger, stronger purpose in life.

Focus on whether you believe in the values of the organization. Does the organization's vision excite you? Are you a better human being because of the resources or culture that organization offers?

Maybe there's a better opportunity out there that aligns well with your vision for yourself, or perhaps a career move that will deliver you an intense sense of accomplishment. That's all well and dandy—make the jump. But I cannot tell you how many times I've seen employees (ahem, millennials) leave an industry for an extra five grand that after taxes yields them a box of tissues to drown their sorrows in.

Think of it this way: no one wakes up and says, I can't wait to go to work and make a hundred thousand salary!

You wake up excited because there's something much bigger at play that you're setting up to accomplish. That's living. That's the type of mindset we need all employees and individuals to adopt to sustain success in both aspects of life. Personal and professional.

Now for you, employers.

The time has really come for us to make a fundamental change in how we're approaching our workplaces.

If you've made it this far into the book and decided not to adopt the ASA Way, I implore you to at the very least recognize there's no way to neatly compartmentalize and separate professional and personal lives. Acknowledge that empowering employees on a personal level will lead to more productive employees, productive teams (and yes, higher revenues). The days of being uninterested in employees' personal lives or making it taboo for employees to express their personal challenges are numbered, if not already passed.

The workforce has changed, the game has changed, employees' mentalities have changed. Most of my employees are millennials or young lawyers who have recently gotten married or are just starting families. I know a thing or two about this younger workforce. And make no mistake, they will not hesitate to drop a dysfunctional employer the first opportunity they get. Notice I did not say organization. I said employer. You've probably heard, but it's worth emphasizing: employees don't leave organizations. They leave leadership. They leave you. And they do that when they no longer believe in you. In fact, a third of millennials today in the workforce are willing to take time off with no plan B, meaning they'd rather say, "Fuck this," walk away from a job with no backup plan, and sit on their ass at home, binge-watching a TV series while they contemplate where they're headed and what they want to do with their lives!

We can either adapt to these times or crumble resisting the change. Like I said, this process does not require a lot of financial capital, but it does require human capital. It requires you to dig really deep within yourself and realize that it's not about you. It's about them, your employees.

The change starts and ends with you. So let's make a conscious choice today to be different as employers, to empower employees, to make our workplaces more dynamic, and to not only be more in tune with the personal challenges our employees face but also provide resources to help them overcome those challenges. I promise you, you'll see the effects in your productivity and growth.

A Final Message for All

These final thoughts are for you: employer, employee, individual, dog walker, mom, CEO, sister, janitor, anyone who's willing to listen. The workplace needs to change, and that change will start with you. It will require a top-to-bottom approach. It will require employees to do their part. It will require employers to do their part. Everyone's going to have to roll up their sleeves and roll in the mud together.

Here's why.

The workplace needs to change, and that change will start with you.

You could have an employer giving the ASA Way their all and offering a whole fucking universe of resources, but nothing positive will come of it if employees aren't taking advantage of those initiatives and capitalizing on those resources to meld into the best iteration of themselves that they can possibly be. And vice versa. Employees can be out there busting their asses trying to improve, but if employers are too busy to give a shit because they're focused on the bottom line, they're impeding change.

We're in this tug-of-war together. Everyone must pull their weight, or we all fall down.

If you're ready to roll, I applaud you. I really do. Let's start by moving beyond the superficial conversations about weather to learning about one another as humans—people who have families, challenges, and lives outside of the office. Let's mean what we say and care about one another to the core. Let's put our Human Being hats on and genuinely look out for one another and help each other grow. Let's adopt the ASA Way.

Will this be easy as pie? Absolutely fucking not.

But guess what? Most things in life that are worth it are difficult. But the rewards are life changing. You can sleep peacefully at night knowing you made a difference in the life of another person, knowing you're living a life of fulfillment, knowing you're in the driver's seat and navigating purposely through life and not just coasting through it by chance.

All of these things, I believe, would make my naani smile.

About the Author

Prior to launching ASA Law Group, LLC, Shuaib Ahmed represented clients in personal injury and medical malpractice cases, served as an Assistant Attorney General for the State of Illinois, and spent numerous years engaged in private practice defending clients in workers' compensation cases.

During his tenure as a partner with a prominent law firm in Chicago, Shuaib realized that the industry was changing while firms remained stagnant in both their litigation approach and internal leadership. Shuaib was determined to create something different. The ASA Way comes from the lessons he learned being raised by his maternal grandmother coupled with his experience in the legal industry. He implemented this high-level thought leadership approach in forming ASA Law Group. What started as a one-man firm has, in less than five years, grown to over twenty employees and scaled into California.

Shuaib attributes this growth to his uncompromising commitment to the ASA Way. Aside from being an entrepreneur, Shuaib is an investor, author, faculty member, and board member of the Business Advisory Board for the Illinois Chamber of Commerce and Kids' Chance of Illinois. His most rewarding job is being a father to his lovely children.

www.ingramcontent.com/pod-product-compliance
Lightning Source LLC
Chambersburg PA
CBHW020455100426
42813CB00031B/3366/J